Presented To:

_____

From:

_____

Date:

_____

the POWER *of* IMAGINATION

Books by Kerry Kirkwood

The Power of Blessing

Available From Destiny Image Publishers

the

POWER *of*

IMAGINATION

Kerry Kirkwood

DESTINY IMAGE® PUBLISHERS, INC.

P.O. Box 310, Shippensburg, PA 17257-0310

"Promoting Inspired Lives."

This book and all other Destiny Image, Revival Press, MercyPlace, Fresh Bread, Destiny Image Fiction, and Treasure House books are available at Christian bookstores and distributors worldwide.

For a U.S. bookstore nearest you, call 1-800-722-6774.

For more information on foreign distributors, call 717-532-3040.

Reach us on the Internet: www.destinyimage.com.

ISBN 13 TP: 978-0-7684-0314-5
ISBN 13 Ebook: 978-0-7684-8812-8

For Worldwide Distribution, Printed in the U.S.A.

4 5 6 7 8 9 / 23 22

IN LOVING MEMORY

It is with great emotion and joy that I write this dedication to my Mother, Vada Faye Kirkwood, who always told me I would write books. If it were not for her ability to endure ridicule and her faithfulness to Christ, I would not have known such love. She faithfully took her children to church every time the doors were open. Whether the weather was pleasant or not, she was there with her kids in tow. To this very day, I miss her reading to me from the Song of Solomon. Her imagination inspired me to see God in bigger light and revelation than the nominal perspective. She gave me her legacy of love for the Word of God and the freedom to believe for the impossible. Many times I saw her pray in needed finances.

Her creative ideas and thoughts not only live on through her children but are expressed in many different ways. She was way before her time in understanding the Power of Imagination. Her sense of balance caused me to weigh everything with the Word. Her love and enjoyment of family lives on through the generations. She is experiencing all heaven has to offer.

ACKNOWLEDGMENTS

Anyone who has ever written something for publication knows the team effort that goes into a project such as this one. I am grateful for all those who have directly and indirectly influenced this message. You will never know the encouragement you passed on to me by your friendship and the faithful purchasing of materials. Your purchase of this teaching series on CD prompted me to take the next step in writing this book of the same name. Your emails and testimonies, some of which were added in the telling of this book, were, in part, the impetus for moving ahead with this painstaking process called writing.

My wife, Diane, who knows my strengths and weaknesses better than anyone and still loves me, has been my partner in this project. Without her prayer and loving support it would have lagged short of completion. Her joy in loving the Lord Jesus Christ with all her heart still urges me to go deeper into His presence.

It is not a stretch when I mention my children who have on numerous occasions said, "I am proud of you, Dad, not because of the book, but because of who you are." Everything we say becomes a legacy; and the longer I live, the more I realize how powerful our words of blessing really are. Thank you Kevin, Casey, Kristen, and Kara. I love you all—you are truly great visionaries.

My special thanks to Kathy Smith, who worked diligently to compile materials from my teachings. She gathered them into a format so I could express this message. Thanks, Kathy, for all the long hours.

I would be remiss not to mention Trinity Fellowship Church in Tyler, Texas—the church we founded in 1987. This church family has been a proving ground for much of what is in this book. You have spurred me to excel, and your love and support has always been overwhelming to Diane and me. Since you have been such "meat eaters" when it comes to the Word of God, I have been challenged to heartily eat of the Word myself.

The staff of Trinity Fellowship is incredible. You have been the biggest cheerleaders and have taken up the slack when needed without complaint. I have never worked with people who have exhibited such servant hearts like you. Duane Hett, thanks for the technical support that was crucial to finishing this manuscript. You are the best executive pastor any senior pastor could ask for. Jim Hahn, I could not have survived the rigorous schedule without your gifting. Jim has carried the load of pastoral care and has covered the pulpit with excellence in my absence. Leah, your skills as a worship pastor and in the office are greatly appreciated. Thanks to the eldership team for allowing me to do what God called me to do. You have played a huge part in the distribution of this message.

*I pray that the eyes of your heart may be enlightened,
so that you will know what is the hope of His calling,
what are the riches of the glory of His inheritance
in the saints* (Ephesians 1:18).

Table of Contents

FOREWORD

When I was a new Jewish believer in Jesus, I avoided anything related to the supernatural power of God. Why? Because it reminded me of what I had experienced during my time in the New Age movement. I had seen healing, meditation, and answered prayer by New Agers, and I wanted nothing to do with anything similar in Christianity. As a result, the devil had me coming and going. He had me trapped in deception *before* I turned to Jesus, and then he made sure I was powerless *after* I came to Jesus.

Gradually, as my mind was renewed by the Word of God, I realized the devil is not original. He is a counterfeit artist. A counterfeiter would never make a three-dollar bill. He makes counterfeit money that is as close to the original as possible. Just because the devil imitates the power of God does not mean we should reject the power of God. *Christianity devoid of the supernatural is just another "religion."*

The nearer we get to the return of Jesus, the more we will need all the supernatural power of God that we can get. Also, it's crucial in these end times that we discern the counterfeit from the authentic. My grave concern is that many of those who never experience the authentic supernatural of God will accept the counterfeit.

A major area that has been hijacked by the devil is the *power of imagination*. Kerry Kirkwood has restored this major biblical revelation. This book will convince you that the power of imagination is biblically authentic, teaches you how to achieve your destiny and healing, and how to receive revelation the same way Jesus did.

I am convinced that Kerry's teaching is a key revelation that will cause the promises of God to manifest in your life. No more will you be confined to being a spectator. You are being called to participate in the greatest release of God's Spirit and supernatural power in the history of planet Earth!

Sid Roth
TV Host, "It's Supernatural"

INTRODUCTION

I f you have ever had a dream or a vision, you are using your imagination. As a child, I was told I had a wild and vivid imagination. Imagination is one of those words that the New Age movement has taken and perverted. Christians, for the most part, have shied away from this term because we have not understood that it was God who created us to have an imagination at creation. God created us in His imagination. He said, *"Let Us make man in Our image"* (Gen. 1:26). He used the plural form when He described who was present at creation. The Father, the Son, and the Holy Spirit were present at creation. The image or DNA we were created in is part of the Trinity. Being created in the image of God means that God thought or determined, and then He formed man.

Man was first seen or imagined by God, and then God completed creation by forming us from the dust of the earth and His breath. We carry the same creative gift. Through the Holy

Spirit we see with our spiritual eyes what God wants to do, and then we are able to move in faith to act.

After the fall of Adam, every part of their lives flipped upside down. Before Adam and Eve's disobedience, their spirits dominated them, and communication was much easier because they did not have to filter everything through a dominant mind. After eating from the tree of the knowledge of good and evil, their eyes were opened to see things through their analytical souls, which is what we call the mind. Adam became dominated by his mind, but his spiritual imagination was still part of his spiritual creation—like all of humankind.

This book shows how you can strengthen your God-given imagination in a balanced, biblical way. If there is a vain imagination, then there must be an original, holy imagination. The devil can only pervert what God created, because the devil has no ability to create.

Imagination simply allows us to see what the Father has already made available for us. Ephesians 1:18 tells us that the eyes of our hearts will be *enlightened* so that we might know the hope of our calling. Enlightened is translated as *photizo*[1] from which we get the word photograph. Imagination is allowing the Holy Spirit to develop a photograph upon our hearts of our potential destinies. The devil wants us to be blind to what God has thought and determined for us.

In this book, you will learn the power of magnification. It is a tool that, when applied to every situation, changes your outcome and your environment. *To shrink the problem, you must magnify the solution.* When the problem becomes greater than the solution, the outcome is unfavorable. Therefore, you will learn how to magnify what God is doing and who He is—then you can watch the favor of God start moving in your behalf.

When God wanted to show Abraham the potential of his generations, he took him outside. God said, "Look up and count the stars; this is what your seed looks like" (see Gen. 26:4). The Father really wants us to be able to see beyond our momentary circumstances. Apostle Paul said what we see is temporal and what we don't see is eternal (see 2 Cor. 4:18). What we see can cause us to miss what we cannot see, which is far greater than what the natural senses can define.

You will learn from this book how to discern between vain imagination and godly imagination. You will be able to separate carnal thinking from Holy Spirit thinking. Paul said that we have the mind of Christ. This tells me that inside all of us is the ability to have the thoughts of the Spirit. Paul taught us to combine spiritual thoughts with spiritual words (see 1 Cor. 2:13). Imagination connects these two so that our words match the thoughts of the Spirit. Meditation is not a New Age concept, but was given to us by God to nourish our spirits so we would have good spiritual health.

If you were to enter my home, the first thing you would see is my family. Not sitting in chairs, but in pictures hanging on the walls. You would get a good sense of our family history. There is a black and white photograph of Diane's Dad dressed in his World War II uniform. If you walked around the room, you would see our children in their elementary stages. Now, we also have pictures of the next generation—our grandchildren. These pictures tell a story, and they allow me to imagine what my children and grandchildren can become.

Words paint pictures in our minds, and pictures point toward destiny. On my smart phone, I have about 100 pictures—they remind me of what I am thankful for. Anytime I get a picture that doesn't fit who I am, I can delete it at the press of a button. As you read this book, allow the Holy Spirit to develop what He wants you to see and delete anything that has been hurtful and a hindrance to you. If you can see what your Father envisions for you, then you can see it come to pass.

Fixing our eyes on Jesus, the Author and Perfector [Finisher] *of* [our] *faith...* (Hebrews 12:2).

Endnotes

1. Bible Study Tools, "Photizo—New Testament Greek Lexicon—New American Standard," Bible studytools.com, http://www.biblestudytools.com/lexi cons/greek/nas/photizo.html, (accessed November 25, 2011).

CHAPTER 1

IT ALL DEPENDS ON HOW YOU SEE IT

When God spoke these words to me, "It all depends on how you see it," I was in a plane flying over the frozen tundra of the Arctic Circle.

Inuvik is probably one the most unlikely locations for a vacation. It is located 26 degrees above the Arctic Circle on the Mackenzie Delta in the Northwest Territory of Canada. It is called the land of the midnight sun, because there is no sunlight the whole month of January. People go for months with little or no sunlight at all. Then, in the summer months of June and July, they experience 24 hours of constant sunshine.

Temperatures in that region have been known to dip into the minus-60-degree range in those brutally cold, dark winter months. Even the polar bears go south for the winter! Once I even saw a sign that read, "2000 miles to the North Pole." Let me tell you something—even Santa doesn't live there! I'm sorry to break that myth for you, but he simply doesn't.

This is truly a land of sharp contrasts. Inuvik is nestled in close to the Arctic Ocean between the magnificent Richardson Mountains and the treeless tundra. The Government of the Northwest Territories (GNWT) Bureau of Statistics listed the population of Inuvik at 3,451 in the year 2000.

So what on earth was this pastor doing on a plane flying high over the Arctic Circle? Trust me, I was not on vacation. Why leave the warmth and the sunshine of Texas to visit the brutal cold awaiting me in Inuvik? It is simple: I was invited. The people of Inuvik invited me to minister to them in the region. They wanted the opportunity to experience all that God had to offer them.

From the very first visit, I found myself falling in love with the people of Inuvik. They had an insatiable hunger for the things of God. Their weather may be extreme by our standards; in fact, by most anyone's standards! But so is their pursuit for the deeper things of the Spirit.

This territory is plagued by high rates of suicide and alcoholism. But if you didn't see the sun for months on end, you may be depressed too. I knew there were many people there who needed to hear the Word of the Lord. There were many who needed to experience His touch. Others simply needed an encounter with Jesus. As I flew over the desolate, lifeless terrain of the tundra, I heard the Lord speaking to me, "What do you see?"

I looked down at miles and miles of ice. Pure desolation enveloped by the frigid cold and a bleak, dark, and foreboding terrain. Much to my surprise there was an element of raw beauty that escaped the desolation, a sharp contrast to everything else that I could see. What did I see? "Not much!" I answered.

"It all depends on how you see it," He responded.

It's all in how you see it. What was it that God could see that I could not? It was there upon the plane high over the Arctic Circle that God began to reveal to me a most profound truth that is the basis of this book.

What Do You See?

It's what we can't see that is most harmful to us. The Scriptures tell us, *"Where there is no vision, the people are unrestrained"* (Prov. 29:18). Without vision, we lack purpose and direction, which implies a mindless wandering. This can often lead to a loss of productivity and an inability to complete tasks. On the other hand, when we have vision, we have the ability to see as God sees and all the endless possibilities.

> *Then God said, "Let Us make man in Our **image**, according to Our likeness; and let them rule over the fish of the sea and over the birds of the sky and over the cattle and over all the earth, and over every creeping thing that creeps on the earth." God created man in His own image, in the image of God He created him; male and female He created them. God blessed them; and God said to them, "Be fruitful and multiply, and fill the earth, and subdue it; and rule over the fish of the sea and over the birds of the sky and over every living thing that moves on the earth"* (Genesis 1:26-28).

That word *image* can also be translated as "in our imagination." We do not usually think of God as having an imagination. In the original Hebrew text, the word image is *tselem*[1], which means a shadow of or resemblance or representation. We know that He was not referring to God as looking like us physically, because the Bible says that God is a spirit. However, the resemblance is our spiritual makeup. We were also created with an imagination. Before the Fall of Adam, man operated in a godly imagination; and after the Fall, he lived with a vain imagination.

Jesus, the second Adam, came and restored us to our Godlike resemblance of a godly imagination. We now have the potential to mature into an imagination that is creative with prophetic insight.

God said, *"Let Us make man in Our image, according to Our likeness; and let them rule over the fish of the sea and over the birds of the sky and over the cattle and over all the earth, and over every creeping thing."* Yes, we are even to rule over the creeping things. We are to do this out of our image, out of our imaginations.

The word *created* in verse 27 and the word *make* in verse 26 are two distinctively different words in the Hebrew. The word *made* means to form out of a substance that already exists upon the earth. The word *created* means to form from a substance that does not exist upon the earth.

When God formed man from the dust of the earth, He made physical man—he was a body but not a being. The second level of creation occurred when God breathed into the body the substance that did not exist upon this earth, which was God Himself. He breathed into man and resuscitated him; man became a living being. We carry the spiritual DNA of God. The inner self is the part that is the resemblance of God the Father. He has breathed into us the sensitivity to be like Him, and we also carry an imagination of the Spirit.

I like what Pastor Olen Griffing says about this original text. "When God breathed into man, he became a speaking spirit. He created us more spirit than he did physical. In the garden before the Fall, God created man with the ability and understanding to communicate with Him on a spiritual level."

I know that God wants us to understand and know Him in a way that does not have to be cerebrally processed or rationalized. In Psalm 50:21, God is speaking to man and He says, *"You thought that I was just like you."* We assume in our rational thinking that if we are having a bad day, then God must be feeling the same way. We think that because we like something that God would like it, too. This is not necessarily true. He created us to understand Him in a spiritual fashion. Our view is sometimes filtered through our culture or society. When we see God through the filter of the Word of God, we can mature in our image or imagination of Him.

That is not New Age woo-woo or a revelation that no one has ever thought of before. We must understand that God has an imagination. In most contexts, many think having an imagination is a bad thing. I was raised with this thinking; people would say, "Oh, you have a *wild* imagination."

The liberal exercising of one's creative imagination is often-times met with a negative response from others. An imagination can trigger sharp criticism and negative feedback as if it is something undesirable and should be discouraged. An imagination that is working on the dark side, in a carnal, lascivious fashion in terms of fantasy and pornography, is not the imagination of God but a perversion of God's divine nature. The devil wants to stop your creativity by causing concern about imagination. There is power in imagination; it just depends on what we are drawn to imagine.

Those who use their God-given creation to go after destructive uses do so by their choice of desire.

Our Creative, Good God

There is one thing that we need to understand: everything began with God and was created good. Before the Internet was invented, God had already thought of it. Everything that began with God was pure; only after it was created could the devil corrupt it. The devil is not omniscient nor is he creative.

For instance, we know that marriage is holy so that is why the devil attempts to break up families. What God puts together is creative and is resistant to evil. Think how powerful it would be for a couple in covenant with God to both be using their creative imagination. Two are better than one, Proverbs tells us. Take dancing, for example. God gave dance as an expressive art for worship. When worship is expressed through someone gifted to dance, the beauty of holiness is seen. When dancing is taken to environments to express lewdness and perversion, then the imagination that was to be used to express worship has been polluted. Because of the pollution of dancing, some churches have decided that it doesn't fit. We should not allow something once sacred to be lost because of perverted imaginations.

If there is a vain imagination, then there must also be a holy imagination.

If we see something as unholy, then that indicates there had to be an original that was holy. If it is unholy now, it is because it has been polluted and used for evil desires. I believe the Lord wants to restore the imagination that Adam had before being exiled from the Garden of Eden.

> *Therefore repent and return, so that your sins may be wiped away, in order that times of **refreshing** may come from the presence of the Lord* (Acts 3:19).

Repentance in this text means to change the way you think about something. It does not necessarily mean to repent over some act of sin that was committed; but if I am thinking in some adverse way to the way of God, then I need to change the way I am thinking and adjust my thoughts to match His.

Repent and be converted are two entirely different things. I cannot be converted or make a directional change until there is a change of thinking. Proverbs shows us that the way a person thinks influences what he becomes. Changing the way we think will change the direction we are going. In Acts 3:19, the word refreshing is similar to the word in Genesis 2:7 when God breathed into man, resuscitated him, and he became a living being, a speaking spirit, a communicating spirit

> *whom heaven must receive until the period of **restoration of all things** about which God spoke by the mouth of His holy prophets from ancient time* (Acts 3:21).

In Revelation 21:5, Jesus said He *is making all things new.* What "things" is He going to make new? What is it that He is going to restore? Notice He did not say He is going to make new things, but make all things (previously created) new. Adam had such an imagination in the Garden that he was able to name all the animals. There will be a time when the imagination that Adam had will not be a vain imagination—but a holy imagination once again.

Through the power of his imagination, Adam was able to communicate and to intuitively know God. Part of the resuscitation that God wants to restore into our lives is in the area of a spiritual imagination about Him. When it is grounded in godliness, we can begin to imagine all the things that God has given us.

> *Now we have received, not the spirit of the world, but the Spirit who is from God, so that we may **know the things freely given to us by God*** (1 Corinthians 2:12).

We know from Ephesians 3:20 that what He can do abundantly exceeds what I can ask or think, *"Now to Him who is able to do far more abundantly beyond all that we ask or think, according to the power that works within us."*

The problem is that my thinking is still part of the fallen nature. I think to myself, *Will God really do this?* Why do I think that? Because it has been my experience that God normally does not do it. Therefore, I limit what God will do because my image of God is that He doesn't do that.

God wants to recreate within us our image of not only who He is, but also our image of who we are in terms of the reflection of who He is through us. Imagination is so strong that it is like a projection screen; once you take hold of the image, the picture becomes indelibly imprinted upon your mind. It is like a template that is burned into your consciousness.

That is precisely why pornography is so strong. It burns an image into the mind that is counteractive to the image of God. Because it is not real, it is not even God. Satan will do anything he can to create an imagination that will take you into another world—out of the Kingdom of God.

Godly Imagination Is Powerful

Godly imagination is so powerful it allows us to receive things beyond what we ask or think. It is according to the power that acts within us. Our imagination can take us beyond the blockage that the enemy has constructed through thoughts that blind our spiritual eyes. The reality of who we are in Him is more real than the deception that the enemy has portrayed by saying "Did God really say that?"

It is interesting that Jesus said, "Come unto Me as little children." Children often have the strongest imaginations. They have the liberty to release the images and thoughts of their imaginations without constraint. Kids can tell you some of the wildest things.

To demonstrate this point, the following are two true stories: Betty and her husband were in charge of a children's home in Texas. Betty recounts the many miracles that took place among the children they cared for. Since the facility was not well funded, they had to rely on donations from the community. Food was scarce many times and choices were few. One day a young girl told Betty, "I really want to eat a T-bone steak." Betty asked her if she had ever eaten one before and she said, "No, but I have heard about it, and I think it would be a good thing if I could have one."

Betty, as most of adults, did not want the young, impressionable girl to be disappointed, so she told her, "Honey, T-bone steaks are expensive, and we should be thankful for what we get." The power of that child's imagination acted with her faith and a couple of days later, someone came to the home and donated enough T-bone steaks for the whole campus to eat. Another time, a child said, "I wish we could have some Captain Crunch cereal." Betty's husband said, "I would rather have some Raisin Bran." Well, you guessed it. In a few days when the donations of food came in, there was cereal in the lot. However, there were only two kinds of cereal—Captain Crunch and Raisin Bran.

When we allow the simplicity of seeing by faith, reality can follow. For some of us, the fear of being disappointed keeps us from allowing our hopes to get too high. Imagination brings desires to the surface of our minds so we will permit prayer and declarations of faith to come forth. Jesus instructed us to believe that we have received what we desire when we pray (see Mark 11:24).

God is creative within us because we were created out of the imagination of God. Imagination moves us outside of the constraints and limitations of the physical realm. It puts us into the spiritual reality, a realm that we can actually see with our own spiritual eyes. It is a realm that is out of this world. It is above and beyond all that we can ask or think according to the power that works within us—His power.

If I only move in the realm of what I can ask or think, I am limited in what I believe God can do, so then I will only ask God for those things that I think are possible. But by my spiritual intuitiveness and imagination, the Holy Spirit can come and burn into my imagination, into my spirit, the very thing that God has intended for me! Those things are there—I just need to be able to see them through imagination, otherwise I do not know God has already put my name on them.

> *But their minds were hardened; for until this very day at the reading of the old covenant the same veil remains unlifted, because it is removed in Christ. But to this day whenever Moses is read, a veil lies over their heart; but whenever a person turns to the Lord, the veil is taken away. Now the Lord is the Spirit, and where the Spirit of the Lord is, there is liberty.* **But we all, with unveiled face, beholding as in a mirror the glory of the Lord, are being transformed into the same image from glory to glory, just as from the Lord, the Spirit** (2 Corinthians 3:14-18).

The mind is very limited in what it can believe the Lord will provide. The mind is always thinking in terms of the experiential, "Here has been my experience...." But God says, "I am not going to move according to your experience. I am going to move according to My image. I have an image to uphold." Verse 18 in Second Corinthians 3 says we are transformed into the same image of what we are looking or focused on. The Holy Spirit wants us to see the image of a loving Father who has good things in store for His children.

Where the Spirit of the Lord is, there is liberty that comes to transform us—the freedom to imagine all God has prepared for those who love Him. The transformation is into the image of God. Paul confirmed the transformation that comes by the renewing or resuscitating of the mind (see Rom. 12:2). When the mind allows the imagination to lead by the Holy Spirit, change does come.

Endnotes

1. Bible Study Tools, "Tselem—Old Testament Hebrew Lexicon—New American Standard," Bible StudyTools.com, http://www.biblestudytools.com/lexicons/hebrew/nas/tselem.html, (accessed Nov 25, 2011).

CHAPTER 2

MADE IN HIS IMAGE

*God, after He spoke long ago to the fathers in the prophets in many portions and in many ways, in these last days has spoken to us in His Son, whom He appointed heir of all things, through whom also He made the world. And He is the radiance of His glory **and the exact representation of His nature,** and upholds all things by the word of His power. When He had made purification of sins, He sat down at the right hand of the Majesty on high* (Hebrews 1:1-3).

The writer of the Book of Hebrews explicitly detailed the timing between the prophets of old speaking and the last days. We know that the last days began when there was a new covenant. Since the new covenant, there was a change in how God would speak to us. His Son would now be the exact representation of His plan.

One day, one of Jesus' disciples asked if Jesus would show them His Father. Jesus replied to Philip, "If you have seen Me, you have seen the Father" (see John 14:9). That may have stretched them somewhat, because they knew they could see Jesus at that very moment. So what did that have to do with seeing the Father? Since Jesus is the personification or expression of God, then they were seeing into a heavenly connection.

When I was about ten years of age, I walked to school when the weather permitted. The walk was about a mile from my home. I would pass a small grocery store owned by Eddie Moore. My dad made arrangements with Mr. Moore so that I could come by and spend thirty cents for lunch and a snack after school. There were no credit cards, only another man's word to pay at the end of the month. After school, some of my friends would follow me to the store, and I would get my snack, about a quarter's worth of candy.

After a few days of this routine, one of my friends, Billy, watched how I got my daily dose of sugar. He did the same thing as I did and put his candy on the counter and Mr. Moore told him it would be 20 cents. Billy, looking puzzled, said to Mr. Moore, "I don't have any money. I just want to do what Kerry is doing." The words from the owner rang out like revelation to my ears. He said, "I know his father, but I don't know yours." Feeling sorry for Billy, I asked to have it put on my bill, which I later had to explain to my dad. Dad had a good name in the community for keeping his word.

I am excited to tell you that your Father in Heaven is known throughout the universe for keeping His Word. It will not return void to Him without accomplishing what His Word was sent to do. You and I have His image superimposed on the inside of us; and when we have a need, know without any doubt that He has already made arrangements for our provision. No one else can tag along and get the VIP treatment without knowing Him as Father.

They can't get their needs met and answers by quoting my words or reciting my story. It must be His image coming through in a very personal way.

Christ in you is the hope of glory.

Colossians 1:27 reminds us of a mystery (at least to unbelievers) that *Christ in us is the hope of glory.* Just think of it: these are the last days and the exact representation is inside of us wanting to communicate with us and through us. It is the same today when the Holy Spirit impresses His image on us to daily represent Him on the earth. He wants us to imagine with Him to see the miracles that represent His goodness. Just let your image of Him extend beyond what you think, and you will see Him work miracles through you.

We have been predestined to become conformed to the image of Christ. We are to be conformed to the imagination of God's Son. Paul said that we are to have the attitude of Christ Jesus (see Phil. 2:5). The King James Version of the Bible actually says, *"Let this **mind** be in you."* We are to have the attitude, the mind, of Christ implanted within us.

We have been predestined both to conform to His image and to have His mind or His "imagination." When we conform or follow His form, unusual things happen. Romans 12:2 says that we are to not be conformed to the system of this world. We are continually being pressed to fit into some form. There is a type of conformity, however, that fits those who will be willing to uphold His image.

In the same way the Spirit also helps our weakness; for we do not know how to pray as we should, but the Spirit Himself intercedes for us with groanings too deep for words; and He who searches the hearts knows what the mind of the Spirit is, because He intercedes for the saints according to the will of God. And we know that God causes all things to work together for good to those who love God, to those who are called according to His purpose. For those whom He foreknew, **He also predestined to become conformed to the image of His Son, so that He would be the firstborn among many brethren;** *and these whom He predestined, He also called; and these whom He called, He also justified; and these whom He justified, He also glorified* (Romans 8:26-30).

The "Fear" Factor

Fear is a form of an imagination. The whole idea of fear is to imagine and believe that something that has not happened yet will happen. Job said, *"What I fear comes upon me"* (Job 3:25). So what we imagine comes upon us. The principle that out of the abundance of the heart, the mouth will surely reveal itself is true. When imagination of fear fills the heart, the mouth begins to speak with cursing. People curse themselves and anything else that doesn't fit into their mold.

So if I am living in a state of fear, it is because my unconscious expectation or imagination has set a course for what I see. Fear is prophetic in that it operates from an unrenewed heart. Fear lives from what is happening all around. Imagination works from the inside out.

Worry is meditation going in the wrong direction.

Meditation is setting your mind on a focused thought and ruminating over it again and again. If you have ever worried about something, then you already know how to meditate. *Worry is meditation going in the wrong direction.* Worry is allowing an imagination of distrust to prophesy the opposite of the image of God. We are reminded over and over in the Bible to *fear not.* We live by what we take in through our natural senses. But if God loves us, then what do we have to fear?

Romans 8:31 really fits here: *"What then, shall we say to these things? If God is for us who can be against us"* (NKJV). Sometimes we just need to speak to those things that cause fear and say to them, "My reality is based upon my faith in the Son of God." Then after you have stated your position, begin to meditate and muse upon what you are looking for in the way of change and blessing. Practice pondering the life you believe for.

Young people may wonder whom they will marry. They may wonder what the person will look like. If this is you, allow the Holy Spirit to choose for you. I'm not talking about fantasizing. Let the desire of your heart be known to the Father, who sees in secret and will reward you openly (see Matt. 6:6).

By the same token, the devil uses imagination to create scenarios in the mind. He may create an image that if you step out and move forward in God, then something bad will happen to you. He may also use vain imagination to make you paranoid over what people are thinking or saying about you.

For instance, if I imagine people don't love me and rehearse phantom conversations I think they have about me, I will probably begin to act like I imagine they think of me. Why not imagine that everyone loves me at least until I have real proof to the contrary. It is amazing the difference when imagination is used to bring God's perspective into view. There are thoughts and possibilities that have not even entered into our hearts, but God wants us to enter into His world.

Dreams

Why do we have dreams? Psychologists say that it is because the mind is full and trying to file thoughts or to bring closure to issues of life. We have the promise that our children can prophesy and old men will dream dreams (see Joel 2:28). I believe there is more happening than psychological twisting and turning. Psalm 16:7 says, *"I will bless the Lord who has counseled me…my mind instructs me in the night."* The Holy Spirit can use dreams to print on our spirits things our conscious minds would not dare to believe. Though our bodies are asleep, our spirits are very much awake and in communication with eternity.

While asleep we may be disconnected with the earthly realm, but we are downloading the purposes of God and reloading our souls for battle when we wake. Don't be mistaken about sleep; God is at work to will and do His good pleasure. Dreams can plant images that give us pictures of destiny. Though the mind may not understand them because they are discerned spiritually, nonetheless they are there filed away in our spirits, waiting for the time that we dare to imagine them and bring them forward.

If He can do that, then why can't He indelibly imprint direction for our lives by giving us godly imaginations? He can!

You can use the imagination God gave you to come in the opposite spirit. Instead of imagining that people hate you, imagine they love you, and cast out your fear of people and any rejection that comes with that fear. Since God's nature is love, He wants to develop His image in you so that you see things through the image of love. The perfect image of God casts out fear.

If we can have our imagination fine-tuned to His image, then we will eliminate fear. We will be able to plug into the future and destiny of our lives; we would have what God had imagined for us to have. When our imaginations are released and restored to what God had originally given to Adam, think of the power and liberty that we will then be free to realize.

When God told Abram (see Gen. 15:5) to look up at the sky and begin to count the stars, do you know what He was saying? Imagine what your seed is going to look like. If you can count them and you can see them, then this is going to be your seed.

Some might label you as practicing some Eastern religion meditation thing if you start imagining and meditating. But if God allowed Abram to have a picture that he could wrap his brain around and see what his future would be, then I think we can ask God to do the same for us. Imagine what marriages would be like when people fall in love and are committed in a covenantal way. Instead of imagining your spouse as the enemy, begin to see him or her how God imagined them to be.

When Adam and Eve walked in the Garden, they were covered with the glory of God. Although they were naked, they could not see their nakedness because they were covered with God's light. Eve was lit up; the glory of God covered her. When they looked at each other, they didn't see flesh; they saw the image of God. Everything was filtered through God's eyes.

But when they ate of the tree of good and evil, everything flipped. Man's thought processes led him; He was led more by his thinking and feelings than by the Spirit. Humankind lost the dominance of the Spirit and was ruled by the soul. The soul makes decisions based on the outward appearance of circumstances. Humankind's spirit became suppressed by rational thinking.

I'm not suggesting you need to check your brain at the door. God has given you a brain. But He does not want that to take the place of what He has prepared for you. When they consumed the fruit of the tree of the knowledge of good and evil, the glory of God (Ichabod) departed. Adam and Eve saw each other for the first time without the glory. They saw one another's faults and weaknesses because they were no longer seeing through the eyes of glory.

The first response they had after they were uncovered was to blame. Adam blamed the woman God gave him; in essence he was blaming God for the confusion. Eve blamed the devil over which they had dominion. God had given them dominion over everything in the Garden, even the devil/serpent.

Through the Eyes of Glory

Through the eyes of glory, Adam and Eve were able to see the destiny that God had planned for them. Through the eyes of glory, their imaginations were not limited. Adam named all of the animals without duplication. God gives us imaginations that see through His eyes and allow us to put a name on what we are seeing.

For indeed what had glory, in this case has no glory because of the glory that surpasses it. For if that which fades away was with glory, much more that which remains is in glory. Therefore having such a hope, we use great boldness in our speech, and are not like Moses, who used to put a veil over his face so that the sons of Israel would not look intently at the end of what was fading away (2 Corinthians 3:10-13).

I am telling you that God wants to give us His godly, righteous imagination so that we can understand the hope and the call that He has for us, as mentioned in Second Corinthians 3 when Paul wrote that Moses came off of the mountain of God with his face radiating with the glory of God. He had been in the presence of glory and his face was glowing from an encounter with God. The people who saw it were frightened and wanted Moses to cover up the glory. I believe this was a prophetic statement from God saying you have seen Me in the cloud and fire overhead, now I want to be in you and upon you. The people rejected the offer and spent the next generation outside of what God had imagined for them.

*But their minds were hardened; for until this very day at the reading of the old covenant the same veil remains unlifted, because it is removed in Christ. But to this day whenever Moses is read, a veil lies over their heart; but whenever a person turns to the Lord, the veil is taken away. Now the Lord is the Spirit, and where the Spirit of the Lord is, there is liberty. But we all, with unveiled face, beholding as in a mirror the glory of the Lord, are being **transformed into the same image from glory to glory, just as from the Lord, the Spirit*** (2 Corinthians 3:14-18).

What had glory? Moses' old covenant has no glory because of the glory that now surpasses it. Whatever glory Moses experienced was only temporary. Moses used a veil to cover his face so that the children of Israel might not look intently at the end of what was fading. The glory was fading, so he covered his face that they might not see that his mountaintop experience had faded away.

We are no longer living in a temporary covenant that fades away with time. We have stamped upon our hearts a picture of the cross—but the image of the resurrection is the crowning moment.

Now the image I carry in my spirit is Jesus at the right side of the Father. That image allows me to resist the devil and not believe any of his lies. That image is so real to me that nothing can replace it. In Acts 7:55-60, while Stephen was sharing the good news of Christ, the religious sect became angry and began assaulting him. The Bible says that Stephen steadfastly looked into Heaven and saw Jesus standing in His resurrected position of authority. Notice, that steadfastly means to fixate on. Stephen caught the image of the resurrected Lord. He was no longer focused on the crowd and feeling their rejection. He was more in the Spirit than he was in the middle of a dilemma. Because Stephen had sight of Jesus in all His glory, he could in turn declare forgiveness over the angry crowd. When someone carries the imagination of redemption, it is much easier to forgive those who have the wrong image of us and perhaps of our Father in Heaven.

Removing the Veil

Religion today has put a veil over the face of the Church and told us to not get too excited because these things are only symbolic. God is not symbolic, though we can express things using prophetic symbols, but in reality these are images of the reality of His Kingdom. That veil is kept over the hearts and minds of people today and hinders them from seeing anything for the present and keeps them yearning, waiting for eternity.

The truth is that eternal living in the heavenlies can begin now. You don't have to wait until you die to enjoy the presence of God. He wants to remove that veil right now that hides the image of God from you, the same imagination that He wants you to have.

It takes seeing the revelation of Christ to remove the veil so that the image of our destiny shines through. If Stephen can see through all the noise of an angry mob and still keep focused on the prize, then we too can see past the moment into the heavenly realm.

Jesus Himself explained this exchange in John 5:19. Jesus answered them saying *"Truly, truly, I say to you, the Son can do nothing of Himself,* **unless it is something He sees the Father doing; for whatever the Father does, these things the Son also does in like manner.***"*

When Jesus was on the cross, He was so in touch with the image of God that He knew when the presence of God turned from Him. The presence turned from Him for just a moment because He took all of the sin of the world upon Himself. The Bible says that God could not look at sin, so God turned His back for just a split moment.

Jesus said, *"My God, my God why have you forsaken me?"* (Mark 15:34). How could He know God had turned away from Him? He was created with spiritual intuitiveness so that He knew when God was there and when He wasn't.

Jesus went about doing good and healing the sick because of the imagination of God—the ability to see what the Father was doing. We must learn to get beyond the old mindset that imagination is something vain. It is God-given if we allow ourselves to be centered on the presence of God. You cannot be in carnality and operate in your imagination because it will take joy from your life. Carnal imagination is a thief—it steals your time and your strength. People who are fixed all day staring at pornography are being robbed of the life God intended them to have.

There is a place in God where His image is pinging our imaginations or our spirits. It is like when a cell phone is sending a signal or ping to another phone via a cell tower. The depth of God is calling or pinging our depth to communicate. Our imagination is one way He communicates with us.

You must learn how to discern your thoughts and imaginations.

We must learn how to discern our thoughts and imaginations. If our imagination is not centered on the love of God, it will take us in the opposite direction of our destiny. Complaining kicks in when we are in the imagination of self-pity. Before you know it, we are daydreaming about all the injustices thrust upon us. When our minds take over the controls, they recall offenses from prior decades. We have to take back the reins of negativity and recognize these thoughts did not come from the Holy Spirit but from an unholy spirit.

Second, judge the thoughts by asking yourself, *are these thoughts exalting themselves above what God thinks about me or others?* Second Corinthians 10:5 says we are to pull down speculations that try to be in a higher place than God. *Speculation is the opposite of God-given imagination.* The mind must be under control of the Holy Spirit at all times or otherwise it will start to speculate. When the serpent approached Eve, it was through speculation and rationalization of God's Words. He put forth the questions and doubts, "Did God *really, really* say you would die? Maybe He is trying to keep you from something—after all, look at the fruit and listen to me. It is OK. You will be more knowledgeable about things than ever before." The devil wanted her to imagine what it would be like out of curiosity.

When we allow our minds to consider things outside of God's perimeters, then we are vulnerable for our imagination to take a wrong turn. Doubt kills the pining of our spirits, and after a time we lose the pursuit of God's presence. The Bible says that Adam and Eve's eyes were opened when they ate the forbidden fruit. It didn't mean that their eyes were closed before. They lost paradise due to speculation and doubt, which led to yielding their imaginations to the enemy. Remember, we become servants to whatever or whomever we yield our members or faculties to.

Hang on to the image of who God created you to be. Stick to it and endure the storms and trials that come. Keep within eyesight of the Father and be diligent to guard the holy things planted inside of you.

CHAPTER 3

HOW TO DEVELOP
A GODLY IMAGINATION

I can tell you exactly how imagination set me free from the fear of
failure. I was invited to minister as part of a presbytery team. It
was my first large presbytery. The building was full and the balcony
was packed. People came to hear prophetic words spoken over the
candidates who had been fasting and praying in preparation for the
big event. The two other presbyters were well known; but as for me,
I had not much of a resume. To say that I was intimidated would be
a definite understatement.

My mind began to picture what excuse I would give when I
froze up and could not deliver the Word of the Lord. I smiled,
but inside I was a quivering bowl of Jell-O. I did not want to let
anyone down, much less the Lord. When the first candidate sat
in the seat ready to be prophesied over, I felt the Lord impress
me. I shut my eyes and He said, "Kerry, I love you, son. I am
here with you right now and everyone in this building loves you."
I began to imagine what that was like because it certainly was
not part of my background life experience. He also told me that

47

if I sat there another moment I would be confounded before the people.

Without realizing, I stood to my feet. I looked at the senior leader of the team, and he looked a little surprised but motioned enthusiastically for me to continue. I did not have a plan; I just knew I could not sit there another second and entertain fear of failure. When I took the step and opened my mouth, I was just as interested to hear what was going to come out as those receiving the prophecy.

The word was a little strange, but I knew it was coming from God. I said, "You carry a payload the size of a C130 cargo plane, and your wife is like a copilot. You are going to carry this load all around the world." The audience began to shout out while some cried and others had their heads down. The pastor in charge told the people, "Kerry does not know these people, but I do. This brother just retired from the military where he was a pilot and flew C130 planes. He is now retired but just got a new job flying cargo around the world in C130s, and his wife gets to go with him."

That day the fear of man and the fear of failing dropped off of me. The Father replaced an old image I had of myself always being mediocre and gave me His image of how He sees me. Now I can see through the eyes of a redeemed image, not one of always being disappointed. The love of God overwhelmed me, and I knew that the key for breakthrough was being filled with His love, which casts out fear.

Falling in Love

Do you remember as a youngster the graffiti found on the back of desks, sides of buildings, and in bathroom stalls in school or in gas stations? One might find a heart with the names of two, perhaps unsuspecting, people graphically displayed for all to see. Johnny loves Debbie or Nancy loves Bobby and so on, declaring the love of one for another. We might refer to such displays of affection as "puppy love." As teens venture into the dating arena, the term may change to that of "first love."

Even adults who first begin to experience an emotional attachment to one another often speak of "falling in love." This type of love is not to be confused with the kind of love about to be discussed in the remainder of this chapter. The type of love that I am referring to as the "power of love" in this text is not an emotion, a feeling, or a sentiment.

The "love of God" is the kind of love that the Scriptures tell us has been "shed abroad" in our hearts by the Holy Spirit. Often people will talk of having a love for God, but it may be a type of love that is circumstantial. Fair-weather Christians express their love for Him when all is going well, but let something happen in life and their love wanes. When this happens, it may diminish their love "for" God, but it cannot take away the love "of" God.

Simply put, the love "of" God comes from Him, for God is love. God is Spirit. The Spirit of love is a very powerful thing. It is administrated and imparted by the Holy Spirit. Everything in Scripture revolves around this Spirit of love. The gifts of God work by love.

People may have a gift from God; but without the Spirit of love, it can be very destructive and has no longevity. Although they may have that gift, the fruit of that gift may not be released and fulfilled. If you see people with incredible gifts, yet it is difficult to see the fruit of love or the outward work of the Holy Spirit, then we know the *power* of love has not been released.

*The love of God is being able to see
things through the eyes of God.*

God is Spirit, and God is love. When you see your circumstances, your boss, or your spouse through the eyes of love, you are seeing them through His image. Where there is unresolved anger and hardness of heart, the images and thoughts are seen through a distorted window. When the power of love is filling people's lives, their imagination will not distort the image of God.

You can discern good and evil by describing what you are seeing:

1. Does it encourage you or others?

2. Does it bring a sense of peace or understanding?

3. Does it have a biblical foundation?

We know that we have come into the spirit of love when there is a giving heart, and not just in terms of money. We want to give of ourselves in time, compassion, forgiveness, words of kindness, and not withholding our affection from our own families. When we withhold affection, it is a type of punishment. God is not about alienation; He is about redemption. The spirit of redemption is connected to the spirit of love. God so loved the world that He gave. He did not send an angel to die for us; He sent the express image of Himself.

When we allow the power of His love to be part of our speech and actions, we then can see things through His eyes. If a person treats others with sarcasm and hateful speech, they should not expect to view others with the favor of God. The way we treat others is the same way we view God.

Can we get past the idea that love is just a feeling or an emotion? God so loved that He did not have to feel anything for me. It is a covenant term, and it is by His Spirit. It is just like being filled with the Holy Spirit.

Fruitful Living

What are the fruits of the Spirit? The first one on the list in Galatians 5 is love! The evidence of being filled with the Holy Spirit is not speaking in tongues, although I have taken great joy and delight in my prayer language. The fruit, or the outgrowth, of that Spirit is evidenced by love, joy, peace, long-suffering, gentleness, meekness, and kindness. (See Galatians 5.)

If we understand that love is not an emotion but a spirit, then that means my response to you, and your response to me, is not based on whether you did something good to earn my love. It is all about seeing you and everyone else through the eyes of God, just as a parent sees their beloved children.

Although a child may mess up, parents feel a sense of pity for their child. Why? Because they can see part of themselves in their child; therefore, they have patience and mercy for their child. There is part of God in us, and He sees something, His seed, His DNA, in us; therefore, His image is bringing us to our full, God-given potential if we allow the power of His love to control us.

The eyes of God do not look at where we are; rather, they look at what we can become. Through the eyes of God, the focus is on the potential and not where we are at the moment. The kind of love that is emotional and is based on feelings is all about what is happening at the moment. Without the Spirit of love, which is God Himself, I can love you today, and tomorrow I may not. It is His Spirit of love that must continue to be indwelling and at work showing Him to be stronger than circumstances.

We must go beyond emotional love and live in covenantal love that says whether you do anything good for me at all, whether you reciprocate my giving to you or not, I will not love you any less than how God has loved me.

Love is more than just a feeling, it is a Spirit! God is love.

> For *the love of Christ controls us,* having concluded this, that one died for all, therefore all died; and He died for all, so that they who live might no longer live for themselves, but for Him who died and rose again on their behalf. Therefore from now on we recognize no one according to the flesh; even though we have known Christ according to the flesh, yet now we know Him in this way no longer. Therefore if anyone is in Christ, he is a new creature; the old things passed away; behold, new things have come. Now all these things are from God, who reconciled us to Himself through Christ and gave us the ministry of reconciliation (2 Corinthians 5:14-18).

We see in verse 14 of Second Corinthians 5 that the love of Christ controls us. When you see someone with no self-control, it is a pretty good indication that the love of God is not part of the person's life. When the love of God, which is the Spirit of God, is in complete control, that person will be willing to lay down his or her life for the service of others. What was it that Paul said in Romans 12:1? Offer yourself a living sacrifice? He was not talking about nailing yourself to a cross. People who have surrendered their self-wills to that extent have then ceased to operate in self-centeredness.

Anyone who is focused solely on his or her own personal needs will have difficulty having the mind of Christ (see 1 Cor. 2:16). When we are constrained by the love of God, then we will have the self-control that is produced by that love working within us. The love of God will impose His own constraint upon us.

When people allow the power of love to control their lives, they will view the world, they will look at their families, and they will see one another through the image of God. Instead of judging, they will have compassionate insight into God's will. Angry judgment leads to an uncontrolled mind that will imagine all kinds of suspicion and paranoia. When I see through the eyes of mercy, I know the way things are at that moment are not the way they are always going to be in the future.

Having a controlled mind through the Spirit of love will protect you from having a rogue imagination. It is then that the love of God dissipates fear and rejection and creates an atmosphere of peace that is generated by a sound mind.

Imaginative Communication

Now let us tie this together with the power of imagination. We know that the issue of imagination for some can be very controversial. For instance, in some cultures, the power of imagination has been harnessed to do some powerful but not necessarily godly things. If you look at the Scriptures, everything before man fell was good. God said it was good.

If something is an original it had to have roots in something good. As mentioned previously, satan has nothing that is original; it is all counterfeit. So if there is a vain imagination, then at some point there had to be a godly imagination. If there was a wild imagination, then there had to be a directed imagination to begin with.

Some scholars believe that when God came down to communicate with Adam and Eve in the Garden, the process of communion with man was probably more nonverbal than verbal, perhaps through their thoughts via their imaginations. We must get past the idea that imagination is some random wandering of the mind. Granted, in some cases, where there is no renewing of the mind, it can be a dangerous journey for an unredeemed mind. There is the power of God that operates through imagination and He has given it to us for creativity and communication with Him. Please do not misunderstand. I am not talking about anything close to mental telepathy or any other New Age thought.

If it were not for the imagination of humankind, we would have no witty inventions. The massive arrays of products on the market today are all the result of someone's creative imagination. The product of one's imagination can be either good or evil depending on what they have submitted themselves to.

> *Each one must do just as he has purposed in his heart, not grudgingly or under compulsion, for God loves a cheerful giver* (2 Corinthians 9:7).

Giving and Receiving

We all know the Scripture that says those who sow sparingly will also reap sparingly. It is often used when taking up an offering. This "cheerful giver" Scripture is often used as well. It tells us that we are to give as we have purposed in our hearts or can be "imagined" doing in our minds. True giving begins from the heart of God. He certainly invented the concept, which brought the greatest offering of all. God so loved that He gave the offering of His Son. Next time you give, first ponder in your heart the potential of the seed you are ready to sow; God saw the harvest before He sent His Son to die. You can see through your imagination what the effects of your giving will be.

If we see giving through the eyes of God (imagination), then we would give of our time, our love, etc. according to His imagination. The Bible says God loves a cheerful giver. What does cheerful mean? It means hilarious. It is hilarious because I can see what is coming. Poverty is not coming, fear is not coming, because I see the result of my obedience and it looks like God doing the math—not me.

When we give according to what we are seeing and not in accordance with what we are feeling, then we release exponential results. If you give based on feeling, then the return is limited. Faith is the substance of things hoped for (see Hebrews 11:1). Imagination has substance and allows us to see the hope that lies within us so we can give toward the expectation of what we were seeing.

*I would have despaired unless I had believed that I **would see the goodness** of the Lord in the land of the living* (Psalm 27:13).

In the same manner, God so loved that He gave. If God loves a cheerful giver, then that means He cheerfully, hilariously gave of His own Son. He imagined and had forethought that by the act of giving His Son as the sacrifice, it would once and for all destroy the power of death over the people of God. He saw the Lamb of God (His Son) slain from the foundation of the world. God saw the seed of Christ sown, and He knew it was going to destroy the headship of the devil that caused people to imagine vain things. It would be replaced with a new headship and a redeemed imagination that sees eye to eye with Him. We don't faint because we can see the Good News, the goodness in the land of our living. Can you see what you are looking at happen? See it, give thanks for what you see, and let it become reality.

> *...seeing that **His divine power** has granted to us **everything** pertaining to life and godliness, through the true knowledge of Him who called us by His own glory and excellence"* (2 Peter 1:3).

Because God has given us everything we need, where is it? We know that Christ in us is the hope of glory. I have to conclude that what I need has been deposited inside me or at least the substance to begin the conception of what I need. If imagination has taken us down the path of seeing no way out of a fix, then we become what we see and think. When hope is deferred, the heart grows sick. God intends for us to see His goodness, which is the seed to sow our way out of any problem.

Our Creative Abilities

Fear has torment and torment steers life away from a person's God-given ability to see hope. God has given us the ability to *create* wealth not to *get* wealth (see Deut. 8:18). It is the imagination that gives us the creative ability to change the circumstances surrounding us and to do so in a realm that is totally beyond us. In order to do this, we must quiet ourselves from the torment of fear and without meditating and reporting on how terrible things are.

Godly imagination blesses— vain imagination curses.

Let the Holy Spirit show you God's intentions for good and not evil. Imagination looks to what God has ahead of you. Vain imagination refers to the past and its failures. Godly imagination blesses—vain imagination curses. It is up to you which way you lean.

Some parents use a graphic method to make a memory in their children by saying something like, "If you run in front of that car, you will be splattered all over the pavement." Parents instill in their children a healthy respect for the streets by giving them an image of what will happen if they disobey. If we can graphically impress our minds that God is good and the devil is bad, there are exciting plans for us if we dare to believe and see them. We become what we behold. What comes into what we hold on to? Holding on to grudges causes us to come into the same spirit we hold to. A curse only comes due to a cause.

Proverbs 26:2 says that we are susceptible to a curse because of our own cursing. I like the way James described the connection between the image of God and the imagination of His kids, *"Every good thing given and every perfect gift is from above, coming down from the Father of lights, with whom there is no variation or shifting shadow"* (James 1:17).

This verse describes God as the Father of illumination or lights. When we are living free from guilt and condemnation, He will light up our understanding so we can recognize the gifts He has made readily available when we see them. In Second Kings 4:2, there was a widow who was in dire straits due to debt. The creditors had already come to take her two children for servitude to pay off the debt. She appeals to the prophet Elisha and said to him, "I have nothing but a little jar of oil." In her eyes, it was nothing, but when illumination came, nothing became the substance for abundance and the way out of debt and recovery of her family.

The Father of illumination wants to reveal ways of freedom beyond the usual ways of looking to someone else to be your provider. Inside you is everything you need for your escape, but it takes a loving relationship with the Father of lights.

Other creative methods of talking to one another include, "You better go on to school, or you won't get a good job," or "You better get a job, or you will have to live on the street," or "You better change your ways, or you will end up in jail!" Our words create images that predict little hope of any change. We use creative imagery to paint pictures all the time—negative and positive.

Why not use this same creative imagery to tap into the Word of God. We know that faith has substance and words create pictures and pictures lead to destiny. If you don't like the channel you are viewing, then change the picture you want to behold so you can become something different. Notice in this next verse how communication affects the outcome of expectations.

The Lord said, "Behold, they are one people, and they all have the same language. And this is what they began to do, and now nothing which they purpose to do [KJV: which they have imagined to do] *will be impossible for them* (Genesis 11:6).

God decided to visit a group of people who lived in a region called Shinar. There was only one language spoken in the whole earth at the time. They used creativity to build a tower into the heavens to make a name for themselves. It was their pride that impressed them to do this. God knew that due to their unity in language and purpose, nothing that they *"imagined to do"* would be withheld from them. The power of unity and one language was so powerful in them, that anything that they would begin to imagine would become reality.

Imagination Becomes Reality

In the eyes of God, imagination is so powerful that it can become reality. There is a place in the Kingdom realm where everything happens far beyond what we experience with our natural senses. Angels move at the speed of light because they are angels of light. Things happen so rapidly and so quickly that our minds cannot compute it. So in the terms of the Kingdom of Heaven, reality is operating in the currency of imagination.

To us, imagination is like some Disney film. Whereas in the beginning, thought was just as strong and understood as speaking. We communicate across the world now not using wires but using light bouncing off satellites (sate-lights). Eternity moves at the speed of revelation and illumination. It is much quicker to see than speak. A picture is worth a thousand words. When we do get a picture or image from the Father of lights, we are to make it known by speaking, which is to reply to Heaven, "I got it loud and clear." We can do this through the prayer of acknowledgment or through thanksgiving. It moves the illumination from our spirit onto the drawing board of this physical realm.

Jesus stated that His Kingdom was not of this realm. He was not in denial of the earthly realm; He just got His illumination from the eternal realm of light. Jesus said He did what He saw His Father do. Which father was He referring to? It is clear He was referring to the Father of Lights.

Allow me to finish the thought concerning the Tower of Babel. In Genesis 11:7, we understand that all that God had to do to stop the progression of their imaginations was disrupt communication. He changed the language, and everything they had purposed came to a halt; and they were scattered, looking for others who spoke the same language. Language draws pictures that lead to destiny.

This next Scripture passage is the crown text of this book. It started me down this track concerning imagination.

> *You have heard that it was said, "You shall not commit adultery." But I say to you that everyone who looks at a woman with lust for her has already committed adultery with her in his heart* (Matthew 5:27-28).

Lust means to intently set your mind in focus with craving upon a thing. Jesus is not referring to just a simple gaze, but rather to capturing the picture. The word commit in this verse means to have already begun to move toward it. So God is saying that once we have begun to see a thing and set our mind upon it, there is then a commitment of movement toward that thing.

Think about this for a moment. If it is possible to picture a woman in a way that God would call it adultery, I believe it is also possible to capture a picture of the beauty of the Lord in such a way that it would also come to pass and change our lives. Perhaps we could go one step further without erring by allowing the Holy Spirit to place an illuminated image of what the Father of Lights wants to give us as His heirs.

Now I understand why He told Abram to step outside the tent and look up and take a picture of his seed and those nations to follow. He told him to count the stars and see what He would do far beyond one generation. It is equally possible for a person to imagine that people hate them or that they are going to get cancer and suffer. The physical body responds to our imaginations. So we might as well plug into the light source instead of living in the darkness.

For centuries, the Nicene fathers practiced meditation. Though meditation is not discussed much in our postmodern Christian culture, it is still very beneficial. The Nicenes simply mused and set their thoughts upon a verse of Scripture until it took life in them, much the way the psalmist reflected:

> *Let the words of my mouth and the meditation of my heart be acceptable in Your sight, O Lord, my rock and my Redeemer* (Psalm 19:14).

Let the words of my mouth and the meditation of my heart be divinely connected to the Lord. Things can happen when we focus our thoughts, our intents, and the meditations of our hearts upon the Lord. As a person thinks in his or her heart so is that person.

David confronting Goliath in First Samuel 17 is a great example of how envisioning and imagination works in us. When David arrived at the camp of Israel to take his brothers some food, and perhaps to get a report on how the battle with the Philistines was progressing, David was just in time to hear the taunting. For 40 days, morning and evening, Goliath would present himself as a challenge to the Israelites, along with some other debilitating words. Fear hung over Israel like a dark cloud. *Look at the size of those guys!* They just could not get the image out of their heads. Every time there was a call for a volunteer to go up against Goliath, the giant's words and image flashed through their already fear-torn minds. They were defeated before they ever stepped onto the field of battle.

David had been hanging out with the sheep and had not listened to the trash talk going on between the two armies. David came into the camp with a different image in his heart. He had been singing songs of deliverance and worship unto God. He had added to his arsenal pictures of killing a lion and a bear that had come to take his sheep. David saw Goliath as no different than a big bear. Because David had not absorbed the environment of fear, he was free to superimpose his image upon the giant. His image was in complete contrast to the fear-struck Israeli army.

I believe David saw himself killing the giant before it happened in the eyes of anyone else. David's brothers certainly did not see it. King Saul did not see it but had no other volunteers. David saw it, and declared to Goliath exactly what he saw and would ultimately do. David's image of how big God was overshadowed the image of Goliath.

Let me suggest that you use Psalm 91 as a weapon. You shall abide under the shadow of the Almighty. You might ask yourself, *Under whose shadow or image am I placing myself?*

CHAPTER 4

THE POWER OF MAGNIFICATION

One day as I was listening to the radio in my car, I heard the Lord speak. He said, "Turn down your radio; I want to tell you something." I turned the radio off and listened; He said to me "In order to shrink a problem, you must first magnify the solution. The bigger I become, the smaller the problem becomes. The solution is not in magnifying the problem; the solution is in magnifying My name."

"In order to shrink a problem, you must turn up the magnification of My name," God told me.

What does it mean to magnify the Lord?

I recall one Sunday morning in church, as we were emphasizing the name of Jesus, the Holy Spirit came upon us corporately in a very profound way. We experienced the weightiness of His manifested glory.

There is such a deposit of His goodness when we make His name bigger than the problem. I know that He dwells within us, but at times He wants to come upon us as well. Scripture tells us that when we get into eternity we shall know, even as we are known. My understanding is that you do not have to figure things out through language interpretation or mental deliberation—you just know.

How did you know when you were born again? Did you know because someone shook your hand and told you that you were? No. You just knew that you knew. Once you know, it can't be taken away from you. The understanding is so deep within your spirit that it becomes woven into your thinking. The change is not something that is done ceremoniously, but rather it is the manifested reality of the work of the Spirit as He is allowed to take up residence and express Himself within you.

When the Spirit of the Lord begins to mesh and communicate with our spirits, it becomes an intimate and eternal relationship He planned from the very beginning. He wanted this relationship with Adam and Eve. He went into the Garden and communicated. It wasn't in the sense of human communication; the communication was more in line of Creator with creation. Words could never express the volumes that were spoken. Spiritual intimacy far exceeds any other form of communication that we could possibly engage in. When we magnify (make bigger) our awareness of the Holy Spirit, His imagination in us kicks into overdrive and we can simply muse at all He has done and wants to do in us and through us.

Psalm 16:11 tells us that in His presence is fullness of joy. Fullness (*pleroo*) means there is nothing more that you can put inside; it is full. It has no capacity for anything additional. In His presence is the full capacity for all that we need pertaining to life and godliness. This tells me we cannot receive all He has for us without His presence.

Magnify God, Not the Problem

Moses knew the importance of God's presence. In Exodus 33:14-14, Moses makes a request. Moses told God he didn't want to go without God going with him. Having that awareness allows us to magnify God's will in every matter rather than fearing how big the problem seems to be.

How does God want us to deal with our problems? He said that if we magnify the Lord, we shrink the problem. Psalm 34:3-4 says, *"O magnify the Lord with me, and let us exalt His name together. I sought the Lord, and He heard me and **delivered me from all my fears.**"* The power of magnification is simple. Make the might of God bigger by giving thanks for His deliverance from the problem. Fear is an imagination that can take over easily when we believe our fears can become reality. Instead, allow your faith in Christ to imagine what success looks like. Ponder on the best coming out of the situation you face. Fear tells your enemy he has you against the wall and there is no way out. Magnifying the Lord through praising His name says to your enemy you will not fail; you will magnify the Lord over the problem and succeed.

Too often people deliberate over the problem instead of liberate the solution.

Too often people deliberate over the problem instead of liberate the solution. The word deliberate implies to delay liberation. To be liberated one must join the liberator.

In Second Chronicles 20, King Jehoshaphat was facing down two large nations at the same time, Moab and Ammon. The odds were against Jehoshaphat. After he enquired of the Lord, he had his answer. Notice how God deals with our enemies. Instead of focusing on the enemy and using human instinct, God told him to appoint singers to go out front. The first thing Moab and Ammon would see were unarmed people, but really they were armed with the magnification of the Lord of hosts. The armada of singers was instructed to praise the beauty of holiness. They were told to sing, *"Give thanks to the Lord, for His lovingkindness is everlasting"* (2 Chron. 20:21). When they began to magnify the greatness of the Lord, God caused the enemies to annihilate each other. The power of magnification changes the odds in your favor.

Enlarge Goodness

I had a recurring dream three nights in a row. It was perplexing, because the outcome revealed a fault line in my family for generations. In the dream, I was on the eighteenth green putting for the championship. There was a million-dollar purse for the winner. I was leading going into the last hole. All I had to do was make a six-inch putt. You golfers will understand this feeling. When I putted, I missed the cup, and I felt the defeat and disappointment. I could hear the groans of the crowd in the grandstands.

The next night the same dream appeared. After the third night, I awoke. While I was thinking about how this dream illustrated a frequent scenario in my life and throughout my family growing up, I felt the Lord break in and say, "Go ahead and make the putt and finish the dream."

My first thought was, *I can't go back to sleep and have any control over my dreams. Or can I?* I realized I could imagine the ball going in. Because I knew this was something spiritual that needed to be broken off my life and family, and I knew it was God's will for me to win, I imagined what the victory would feel like. I saw myself making the putt without fear of losing, and I could hear the ball land in the bottom of the plastic cup.

I never had that dream again after that breakthrough. Since that time, I can honestly tell you I have had many successes and no more near misses or sabotage. The fact that I am writing this book is proof of breaking the barrier of failure.

Whatever you enlarge is the very thing that catches your eye and captures your faith to believe.

Whatever we enlarge is the very thing that catches our eye and captures our faith to believe. We can rehearse a problem to everyone we see, and even replay it in our minds so that it magnifies to the point that we accept defeat.

I heard about a construction worker who discovered a bump on his arm. He showed it to a co-worker who told him it looked cancerous. He showed it to someone else who told him it looked just like what a friend had and died. After spending three weeks in torment and fear, he finally went to the doctor. The doctor took one look at it and said it was just a harmless mole and cut it off.

I read an article a few years ago about hypochondriacs. The study showed that 50 percent of medical students began having symptoms of the diseases they were studying. Proverbs says, *"as a person thinks in his heart so he becomes"* (Prov. 23:7). It is easy to see how imagination can work against you—and for you. Consider the problems you can overcome when you magnify the solution more than the problem.

In Numbers 20:7-12, we find that Moses was becoming very frustrated. He was once again caught between God and the people. This time they were complaining because of the extreme conditions in the desert without their thirst being satisfied. They were spreading fear among themselves saying, "Why has Moses brought us to this wilderness except to die?" The grumblers recited how good they had it in Egypt. God told Moses, *"Take the rod; and you and your brother Aaron assemble the congregation and speak to the rock before their eyes"* (Num. 20:8).

Now the first time they cried out for water, Moses was told to strike the rock and water flowed out. It was a covenant type of Jesus being crucified with Christ being the rock. When the rock/Christ was struck, the water or blood came gushing out. The second time the people cried out demanding water, Moses was told to only speak to the rock. But instead of speaking to the rock, he spoke to the people. God never told him to speak to the people; all Moses could see was angry, ungrateful people. Instead of speaking to the rock, which would have given the prophetic image of speaking to Christ our Rock, Moses spoke to the people.

What a perfect example how we could save ourselves anguish if we only would talk to God about the problem first before speaking to the people we think are the problem. His first act was not obeying what God had said; instead he called the people rebels. Though what he said may have been a fact, it was not what God had instructed him to do. The complaining was magnified in Moses' mind over the instructions of God

Obedience—the First Step

Obedience cannot be the second step and still be obedience. In Moses' case, he reverted to past experience and struck the rock as he had done before. Though he got results for the people, he had lost his promise of entering the land he had so desperately longed for.

Numbers 20:12 reveals the heart of the matter. God told Moses that because he did not treat God as Holy *in the sight of the people*, He would not bring the assembly into the land that God had given them. It was the grand opportunity for Moses to magnify and show off the love and greatness of God in front of this entire emerging nation. Instead, Moses magnified his frustration and lack of patience over the mercy of God, and it cost him his promise.

God wants us to take opportunities to magnify His name before the people with whom we have influence. He wants us to go before the people of our city and country as His own personal ambassadors. He wants us to demonstrate this attribute of holiness in our daily lives with our friends and family.

The account of an old priest in First Samuel chapter 2 emphasizes the principle of magnification. Eli the priest was responsible for the spiritual climate. The Bible describes Eli's sons as worthless. They had the reputation among the community as being promiscuous. Their perverted ways overshadowed any spiritual activity happening. At Eli's age, he became complacent with his sons. Though Eli knew of the sexual perversion and the thievery that was being perpetrated by his sons, he did nothing to change their ways and influence on the community. As a result of their lawless behavior, the Bible states in First Samuel 3:1 that prophetic words from the Lord were infrequent and visions were rare. Because they defiled the image of God, they no longer had access to prophetic revelations from God.

Without a fresh revelation of God, we merely go through the pomp and ceremony and fail to experience a demonstration of God's power.

> *Therefore the Lord God of Israel declares, "I did indeed say that your house and the house of your father should walk before Me forever"; but now the Lord declares, "Far be it from Me for* **those who honor Me I will honor, and those who despise Me will be lightly esteemed***" (1 Samuel 2:30).*

The rebuke to Eli was that he had honored or emphasized his sons' ways more than the ways of God. To honor is to glorify or bring illumination upon. We could say that because Eli did not magnify God greater than his sons, he lost the potential of God honoring him in an enduring way. History records Eli's failures and none of his good deeds. Magnification of God brings to pass the promises we have in Christ for ourselves and for our family generations to come.

Psalm 103:7 is an interesting verse. It says that Moses knew the ways of God, but the sons of Israel knew the acts of God. God was telling them He did not want them to merely know of His acts; He wanted them to know His ways.

Israel saw the power of God and even saw the acts of God, but they still did not believe! When it came time for them to enter into the promise, they could not bring themselves to trust God. They failed to enter due to doubt and fear of the unknown. We hear the saying that "seeing is believing." Seeing a display of God's power does not ensure that a person will believe. The slaves who came out of Egypt saw again and again God's demonstration of power and favor, but their years of slavery kept them in hindsight and hindered their foresight.

The ability to imagine what God has for you can depend on getting free from past experiences that, by default, choose for us what we will see. While spying out the land God promised, all but two of the spies could only see the unusual men we now call giants. In their minds, the giants overshadowed them thus diminishing the power of God they had seen displayed many times leading up to this point. Maybe you can remember times when you had opportunities to step into a new day but could not see beyond your past boundaries. The power to imagine beyond what you can even think breaks the auto responses that cause you to decline the offers.

This brings to mind a friend of many years ago. Brad asked for prayer that he might get the dream job of his life. He recited all the benefits of this new position. He even threw in how he could glorify God financially and influence others. He did say that it would be a miracle since there were three other people in line for the superintendent position. I asked him, "Can you see yourself doing this?" He said yes, so we proceeded to ask for favor and the miracle that would be needed.

A couple of weeks later I saw him in church. He couldn't wait to talk with me. He said, "You won't believe what happened." I thought to myself, *If I can't believe it, then why did we even pray?* He laid out the timeline. Unexpectedly the guy in the position he wanted had retired. The second in line transferred out, and the third had taken ill and passed away. He was excited to see how God had given him what he had envisioned. The sad part of this story is that we never again saw Brad in church. He said he was so busy with the new job that he didn't have time to come to service. The point I want to make here is that it is possible to get results; but if we don't know the ways of God, the acts of God become blended into the background of everyday life.

God's Acts and His Ways

The covenantal people of God were missing one crucial element in their preparation for the promise. They had experienced God's acts, but they lacked a personal encounter with God. They knew what He could do, but had yet to meet Him in an intimate way as God their Father. They only knew Him as God their Deliverer. The Word says, *"When a man's ways are pleasing to the Lord, He makes even his enemies to be at peace with him"* (Prov. 16:7).

When your ways please the Lord, even enemies have to stand aside your gate and watch you pass through. God says that He will give you safe passage through the enemy's camp if your ways please Him. The ways of God simply mean how He views things from His perspective.

I can make my demand using the Word of God, and I can say, "Your Word says..." We may even get results, but all the while we are not magnifying the Lord. We are magnifying our own faith and our ability to get it done. The Word without the leading of His Spirit can be a dead letter (see 2 Cor. 3:6).

The Hebrew word for magnify literally means a twisting together like the twisting of a three-fold cord. The word implies the increase of something until it is larger than what is being compared to it.

When Israel entered the Promised Land, they needed to know the God they worshiped and magnified was greater than the Sons of Anak (giants). If they did not magnify their God, then they would have been diminished and appeared to themselves like grasshoppers. When God is magnified, everything in opposition is diminished. The reason Moses was not allowed to go into the Land was because he diminished God in front of the people. To the people, it appeared as if it was Moses who had opened the rock and released the water to satisfy their thirst. God wanted the rock to be seen as their prophetic future when the rock would be seen as their Messiah. Messiah would be struck once and then there would be a New Covenant, not like the old one that could not be kept. In the New Covenant one can speak to the Rock and living water will flow out (see John 16:23). God says, "I want you to learn to speak to the rock. When you get into the land and I am magnified, the giants will not be an issue."

When something is magnified, it becomes a bigger reality than the thing we are facing. Jesus taught us to pray in Matthew 6: *"Thy kingdom come, Thy will be done on earth as it is in Heaven"* (KJV). When we magnify what is happening in Heaven greater than what is happening on earth, then the greater reality is released to come into our circumstance. What we magnify, we permit to rule. Who we magnify is whom we worship.

When we say, "magnify the Lord," we are saying let the reality of His Kingdom take precedence over mine. If there is sickness in my body, and I constantly magnify the doctor's report and the disease and all its symptoms, then I am increasing the disease and diminishing the Healer. If Jesus the Healer is magnified in the middle of the struggle, then we are declaring Jesus is greater than the infirmity. Magnify the Lord with me and let us exalt his name together the psalmist said. This poor psalmist cried out and the Lord heard him. Why did he hear him? Because he magnified the Lord more than what was surrounding him.

Faith is the Substance of Reality

Faith is not just the result of what we feel; it is the substance of reality. In Acts 16, Paul and Silas are in prison. They could have magnified the fact that they were imprisoned unjustly. The pair had the option to complain and reflect how they could have done things differently or they could have played the blame game. Silas could have blamed Paul for making some people angry and putting them in this position. But instead of magnifying their problem, they chose to magnify the Lord. They rejoiced because they were able to suffer for the Lord.

What kind of masochist idea was that? Their reality was not held to the confines of a jail cell. It was not held to people who had maligned them or to Roman torture. Their reality was the glory of God.

> *Let all who seek You rejoice and be glad in You; let those who love Your salvation say continually, "The Lord be magnified!"* (Psalm 40:16).

In Acts 7:55, Stephen was stoned for sharing the Good News of the Kingdom. As mentioned previously, he was not captured by the brutality of the people or anger over the lack of angelic rescue. He refused to magnify the stoning. Instead of addressing those hurling the rocks or focusing upon his circumstances, he chose to look up and catch the image of Jesus standing at the right side of God. Everything changed at that moment. Stephen knew his identity and destiny did not lie with those persecuting him.

Jesus was being magnified many times greater than anything happening on this earth. Perhaps that is the only way that Stephen could say, "Father, forgive them." The stoning became a lesser reality compared to the glory of God. The image of Jesus standing for Stephen was now of greater value and power than anything anyone had ever done against him.

When you magnify the Lord, you are bringing the reality of who He is to influence what is temporarily happening at the moment. Choose the greater glory, and you will always have the right picture in mind. When God's reality becomes greater than the reality of what you are dealing with, then He is magnified. That is what I call living out the *ways of God.*

I find it interesting to also note that scenes of Jesus in Heaven are seen usually with Him sitting at the right side of God. Whereas in the vision Stephen had, Jesus was standing at the right side of God. Perhaps it was a welcoming posture to Stephen; as if Jesus were saying to him, "You are more here in Heaven than there in that crisis." As Stephen went through martyrdom, Jesus stood with him.

Jesus is magnified in my heart when I think more about Him than I do anything or anyone else, when I talk more about the goodness of God than any injustice.

I will give You thanks with all my heart; I will sing praises to You before the gods. I will bow down toward Your holy temple and give thanks to Your name for Your loving kindness and Your truth; for You have magnified Your word according to all Your name (Psalm 138:1).

For as is His name, so is His praise.

For instance, as you praise Him as the Lord of mercy, He shows up as the Lord of mercy. If we magnify Him as Jehovah Jireh, then He shows up as the great Provider. When we magnify Him as Jehovah Shalom, He reveals Himself as our peace. No matter what you are dealing with, set your affection and your heart on the Lord, and not on the problem.

In First Samuel 17 we read the story of David and Goliath. The armies of Israel had heard all the taunts and the threats for 40 days. It came to the point Israel believed what was being said. In fact, it actually paralyzed them and they started believing the imagery Goliath was developing in their minds. When fear captures a home or an individual, all that can be seen is the end game of destruction and failure. The counter to this is to measure the circumstance against Jesus the Word. When you see the problem start to shrink in light of how big God is in comparison to the problem, you know you are on your way to victory.

Because the army of Israel was living in the delusion of fear, they could not move ahead. What did David say regarding the threats of Goliath? He told him that he came in the name of the Lord. That is one huge name. It meant that he had come in the name of the Lord of hosts; you know the one. He is the one and only Lord Jehovah who possesses the whole angelic host from Heaven, and they stand ready to respond to His every command. Who could hope to withstand the army of the Lord? David told Goliath that the Lord Himself would deliver him into his hand.

He was not claiming that he would do it under his own power. David said, "It is the Lord." He is the One who would deliver him into his hand that day. David saw an opportunity for God to be glorified against a giant that Israel thought could not be defeated.

What do you see? When God is magnified, even our enemies are scattered.

My wife, Diane, and I were eating in a restaurant in Houston one evening before going to minister. A waiter came to our table and asked if I was driving a Red Envoy. I was so surprised by the question I paused for a moment to remember what vehicle we were in. Diane said, "Yes, we are." He asked if the window had been broken before we came into the restaurant. When I replied that it hadn't been broken, He told us there was glass all over the ground.

I ran out to see if it was a mistake and soon realized our car had been burglarized. We had all the normal feelings people have in these situations. We felt violated and wondered why our car was chosen when there were other cars in the lot. Diane and I quickly inventoried what had been taken and discovered my briefcase was gone along with a travel bag of Diane's that contained her Bible and a Joyce Meyer book. They probably thought there was a computer in my briefcase, but instead it was filled mainly with my notes—five years worth of study for a book I was researching.

After the police report, we returned to our hotel somewhat defeated. The first thing my wife always wants to do is pray. I thought it was a done deal; even the police said these smash-and-grab thefts are hard to investigate. We started to pray and give thanks that no one was injured and that I had not brought my computer on this trip. Then Diane felt God impress on her that we would recover all our things, and that we were to use First Samuel 30 as a point of faith to stand on.

Houston is an enormous city, and God was saying that we were going to recover the briefcase? That sounded like looking for a needle in a haystack. How could we possibly recover it when we had no idea where to even begin looking? We walked around the hotel room declaring, "God, You are all-knowing and nothing is hidden from You." We began blessing the people who took it. We asked the Lord to let their hearts come into the knowledge of the Son of God. The Holy Spirit dropped the thought into my heart to call my remote answering machine for any messages. I had purchased the answering machine several years before, and I had never used the feature that allowed me to remotely call the machine to get messages. I knew there was a code needed to access the messages. Then I remembered that several years ago I had placed the code in my billfold and to my surprise it was there along with the instructions for the process.

When I replayed the messages, I heard a man say, "Are you Mr. Kirkwood? If you are, please call this number. I have your briefcase." When I called, he explained that he owned a barbershop not far from the hotel where we were staying. He said that he had gone out to empty the trash and the wind had been blowing so hard that he had to walk around to the other end of the dumpster so that the wind would be at his back. There he saw Diane's book, the briefcase, and my notes. He found my number and notes in the briefcase. It just happened that he also was a preacher. By the time we got to his shop, he had cleaned the case and put all the notes back into the briefcase along with Diane's bag. We had recovered everything. The lesson learned that day and every day—God was bigger than Houston, and all problems that come our way.

When He is magnified above the problem, things turn around.

CHAPTER 5

Supernatural Vision

I will stand on my guard post and station myself on the rampart;
*and **I will keep watch to see** what He will speak to me...*
(Habakkuk 2:1).

What do you see?

What is He speaking to your heart today?

Can you see what He is saying?

Habakkuk said that he was going to stand watch upon the wall—for what was he watching? He was watching for the word of the Lord. He wanted to not only hear what the Lord had to say, but he wanted to see it as well. This piques my interest as to how words and pictures fit together. Most would agree that words create pictures and pictures can create destiny.

As a young child, I would dream; not the kind of dream that I needed to be asleep. I would daydream, as some call it. Today I would describe it as imagination. Toy manufacturers use children's imaginations as the fundamentals for designing toys for various ages. Perhaps the reason we are to come to Christ like little children is because we can see with our spiritual imagination easier than when our minds are filled with adult skepticism and pride.

In my daydreams, I always saw myself preaching long before anyone recognized I might be gifted. For me, it began in my bedroom while all my siblings were at school. I would gather all my sisters' dolls, teddy bears, and anything else that looked as if it would pay attention to a young, budding preacher. I imagined the room filled with eager people ready to receive the Word. Since I wasn't old enough to read, I held an old 10-pound Webster's Dictionary in both hands until it was time to point and shake my finger at Teddy Bear, whom I considered the biggest sinner of my flock. I raised my voice to show my authority. I talked about the same things I heard my pastor talk about. I remember that all the dolls and bears got saved every time I preached.

Most parents would agree that a child's imagination is part of the developmental process toward maturity. I also believe that part of the maturity of our faith is to allow the Godlike image He gave us to develop. Maturity is not doing away with childlike imagery. I understand why the Bible teaches us that we are to put away childish behavior. There are some adults who still sport childish attitudes. As I see it, there is a difference between childlike and childishness. I am not suggesting that we entertain childlike fantasy like talking to imaginary friends. However, the Bible is filled with imagery that, on the surface, cerebral thinkers would have trouble accepting.

For instance, God asked Ezekiel the question, after viewing a valley full of dry bones, *"Can these bones live?"* (Ezek. 37:3). The Bible calls it a vision, but nonetheless it is an image of great proportion. The purpose of the vision was for Ezekiel to prophesize over Israel. It was a graphic picture of Israel being placed in the land God had promised. The image stirred Ezekiel to prophesy to the wind and speak over the bones. These images stirred the prophetic words.

There are times when we can prophetically demonstrate what we may be seeing through the imagination that the Holy Spirit prompts.

Creation began in similar fashion. God the Father imagined/thought it, the Son expressed/declared it, and the Holy Spirit carried it out. Originally, Adam and Eve operated in their imagination to communicate with God. The creativity that was upon them to name all the animals came from God. The Scriptures tell us that Adam and Eve were to cultivate or keep the Garden. Cultivate is referring to the oversight. To have oversight, a person must be able to see what it looks like. An architect has oversight because he or she has a picture of what is to be built. Cultivate also means to bring something to pass or to fullness. Sometimes people who are physically blind can see better through their senses than those who have great eyesight.

The thought is first conceived within your heart and then seen within the eyes imagination.

The creative process we use daily is not much different, except ours perhaps is on a different scale. For instance, the apostle Paul said in Second Corinthians 4:13, *"having the same spirit of faith, according to what is written, 'I believed therefore I spoke.'"* The thought first is conceived within our hearts and then seen within the eyes of imagination. Once it can be seen, it must also be spoken. It is spoken into being through faith.

Faith is not abstract; it has substance according Hebrews 11. The word substance is translated *hupostasis,* which means structure. As the architect sees the building he wants to build, he begins with a structure for strength, so after the building is completed it will withstand resistance of the elements. *A thought conceived, believed, seen, and spoken has spiritual structure to build upon.* Ezekiel's vision was a foundation that he could believe, which led him to speak/prophesy—the end result was the fullness of a people who looked like an army. This is the process by which we can see apart from our natural sight. To use natural sight, we need *natural light* to be able to see; with the spirit of our imagination, we need *enlightened light* to be able to see.

> *I pray that the **eyes of your heart** may be **enlightened,** so you will know what the hope of His calling is and what are the riches of the glory of His inheritance in the saints* (Ephesians 1:18).

We have been empowered and entrusted with the most incredible honor humankind could ever conceive of—to be guided by the Holy Spirit. Notice Paul did not say the eyes of your head were going to be enlightened. It says the eyes of the heart were going to be able to see. The word enlighten is huge. The Greek Word is *photizo,* from which we get the word photograph. We could read this verse by saying: the eyes of your spirit may take a photograph so you will know what is the hope or expectation of His calling.

The "eyes of the heart" indicate the idea of imagination. We are a little more comfortable with the word meditation. In the original Hebrew, the word for meditation is *Hagah,* which is the concept of imagination. Meditation may be similar to daydreaming for some. In any case, there can be an image or picture that flashes through your mind at the speed of light—or should I say at the speed of revelation.

In other words, in God's eyes, once conceived and believed in one's heart, a thought is a reality even before it has had the opportunity to manifest itself in the physical realm. Reality can come from believing something so strongly, so intently in your heart, that you begin to act upon what you intentionally believe. Proverbs describes it "as one believes in his heart so he becomes." What you behold, you will become.

Grass and Lilies Test

It is important to keep all of this in a godly perspective and not allow your mind to conceive evil plans. Like prophecy, your imagination needs the filter of the inerrant Word of God. Here is a little test I use to help filter thoughts and determine their origin. I call this the grass and lilies test. First Peter 1:23-24 says we have not been born again with corruptible seed but with incorruptible seed, which is the Word of God. First Peter 1:24 says that all flesh is like grass. Flesh is the thoughts that are not born from biblical seed; and if placed out in the sun for scrutiny, they will quickly wither away.

On the other hand, Jesus said in Matthew 6:28 to notice the lilies. They don't strive to be lilies. They just do what they were created to do—bloom and look beautiful. The bottom line is to not struggle trying to get a picture from the Holy Spirit. He is the one who will do the guiding—He is the film director of what you are to see. Just relax and be a lily. You were created to reflect the image of God, and He will unfold to you what you need to know when you need to know it. Just stay tuned in.

How powerful this would be if we were to utilize this process to bring about change within our families. We understand that faith without works is dead. There can, by the Spirit, be a picture within us of a healthy, happy family that is cultivated inside us waiting for development. If you can see it, you can have it. Once you see it, you will find yourself responding in concert with your internal picture screen.

The reason movies are effective is because the picture and dialogue sticks with us for years. Some people role-play based on what they witnessed in a movie. We remember more of what we see than what we hear; and when the two are put together, memories are indelible. As already mentioned, pornography is so addictive because the pictures and images are burned into the subconscious, deposited for such a time when the devil will replay the images to cause shame and emotional blackmail. Replacement images can be developed after a person has been cleansed from the demonic attachment by asking the Holy Spirit to provide images of God's glory and goodness to reveal what is true.

> *It is the glory of God to conceal a matter, but the glory of kings is to search out a matter* (Proverbs 25:2).

God may conceal or hide something from us, but He does not intend to bar us from receiving it. At times He will create within us the appetite to search out His Word and look for what He has already said we could inherit. Though you see what you believe, it seems to be sealed and you can't get to it; this serves only to raise the craving for its completion.

One of my favorite memories growing up was during Christmas holidays. Part of the festive protocol was the baking. Even after I had my own family, we would go home for Christmas, and we continued the tradition. The routine included my mother making fantastic chocolate fudge a few days before Christmas. I could smell it when I came into the house and the picture of the tray heaped up with fudge drove my senses wild. Mother would hide the fudge until Christmas Day, and the concealing of the fudge only served to raise the delicious expectation for my four siblings and me. The more we thought about it, the more we wanted the fudge. That is when the exploration would begin. We would go hunting for the fudge, looking in Mother's favorite hiding spots.

When we found the fudge, we would eat a few pieces and then re-hide it, leaving a note that said that we loved the fudge so much we couldn't wait for Christmas. We would also include a few clues so she could find the re-hidden delight. The pursuit of the fudge was perhaps as enjoyable as eating the fudge—well, almost. Likewise, God at times conceals something for a time to encourage our pursuit so our hunger and thirst for Him is increased.

Look Where You Are Walking

Remember when Peter walked on the water? (See Matthew 14:22-33.) Peter caught a glimpse of what appeared to be Jesus walking on the water toward the boat. Peter was so excited to see Jesus that all he needed was a confirmation from Jesus that it was truly Him. When Jesus confirmed and told Peter to come to Him, Peter got out of the boat without first considering the laws of buoyancy or weight displacement. Peter had no previous experience in water walking. All Peter had to go on was an image of Jesus on the water. The picture he saw overcame his fear of drowning or any criticism he may have heard from the others in the boat. Peter was focused on Jesus. He submitted himself to Jesus as the Commander by saying, "Whatever You command me to do, I will do."

Not only did Peter have to step out of the boat, he also had to step out of the natural, comfortable realm and into the supernatural realm. Peter was defying all the laws of gravity and wind resistance—until he lost sight of Jesus by looking at the natural circumstances surrounding him. He started to sink when he could not see anything but the boisterous waves. In the boat, he was naturally safe; but when he wanted to go to another level, he had to say, "Lord, I want You to command me." It was the commandment that took him from the natural realm into the supernatural realm.

It is that ability to see, even as our heavenly Father sees, that gives us the confidence to go beyond safe and sound.

Fear will sink you, but Godly imagination will raise you.

We must come to understand that for anything to superimpose itself over the natural law, faith is required. We can choose to live life fearfully, always looking for the next catastrophe, or we can look for the glory in the moment.

As Spirit-filled people, we are filled with the Holy Spirit through which He reveals the image of God to us. Tormenting fear can fill people to the point that they cannot see anything good because their screen is blurred with past failures and they start assuming the future will be the same as their past.

Allow the Holy Spirit to clean the screen and give you a new perspective. The image of Jesus hanging on the cross is an important one—but incomplete. If our image of Christ is based on His death, we have no power over fear. Ask the Holy Spirit for the image of the resurrected Lord, who set the precedent for your success. You are a chip off the ol' Rock. When confronted with fear, replace the torment of fear with the joy of resurrection. *You win!*

It is the power of imagination that stirs our spiritual senses just like the smell of a freshly baked apple pie does to our natural senses. Not only do we have five natural senses, but we posses five spiritual senses as well. Psalm 34:8 tells us to taste and see the goodness of the Lord. The psalmist was not speaking about natural taste or sight.

After Adam and Eve ate from the tree of the knowledge of good and evil, they changed from spiritual dominance to mind dominance. The mind stores the history and experiences of the past, both good and bad. The mind draws from the natural senses for direction and so on. The spiritual senses are not used for recording the past but function to guide us into our hope and future (see Jer. 29:11). Knowing this gives you supernatural realms of faith, especially in regard to family. It is important that you allow the Lord to give you glimpses of what He is making available to you. It is this supernatural vision that will empower you to pray according to the will of God, not just according to the problem.

> *Therefore I urge you, brethren, by the mercies of God, to*
> *present your bodies a living and holy sacrifice, acceptable*
> *to God, which is your spiritual service of worship.*
> ***And do not be conformed to this world, but be***
> ***transformed by the renewing of your mind,*** *so that*
> *you may prove what the will of God is, that which is good*
> *and acceptable and perfect* (Romans 12:1).

We are to love the Lord with our whole hearts, souls, and strength. We are to worship Him with our whole being, every part of our being, and not just our minds. We are not to be molded or fashioned by current trends and culture.

There is a principle in life experience that predicts that emptiness gives opportunity for garbage. For instance, drive by a vacant lot in an inner city and you will find discarded televisions, furniture, and just plain trash. Because the lot is empty, it invites people to put something in it. Jesus taught a similar picture in Matthew 12:43-45. He said that when an unclean spirit is cast out of the house (person), it goes through dry places looking for another host from which to feed from. Then it decides to return to the former host (person) and, finding it clean but empty, moves back in. And because it is vacant, the demon takes seven buddies with it that are even more wicked than the first one. The house is worse than before it was cleaned.

It is not enough just to be clean and empty; we need to be filled with the mind of Christ (see 1 Cor. 2:16). The mind of Christ is the imagination and thoughts of God. Being filled with joy for the hope that lies within you leaves no room for any demons and cohorts to invade. It is possible to live in such wonder and awe of God that you awake greeting the Father and asking what is on the agenda for that day. Empty people wake up and think what a blue Monday it is. Proverbs 29:18 says where there is no prophetic vision, people are unrestrained. This means they have no direction in their lives and nothing to look forward to, so all they have to think upon is what the past dealt them. Where there is no picture to use as a road map, they miss turns and opportunities for success because they have tunnel vision. Empty people expect nothing to protect their hopes from being disappointed.

Solution for Emptiness

Ephesians 5:18-19 is the prescription: *"be filled with the Spirit, speaking to one another in psalms and hymns and spiritual songs, singing and making melody with your heart to the Lord."* Being filled with the Spirit carries a number of levels, but for the sake of this context, I am referring to being filled with supernatural vision to see beyond the circumstances. Joy is the lens cleaner that helps us see the doors of opportunity that exist for us.

Some use the term burnout to describe a feeling, and for some it may be sheer exhaustion. For some, burnout is the lack of renewal after a siege of being spent. Take time to think on promises that the Word of God gives to everyone who believes and acts on His Word.

> *And do not be conformed to this world, but be* **transformed** *by the renewing of your mind, so that you may* **prove** *what the will of God is, that which is good and acceptable and perfect* (Romans 12:2).

Vision allows you to live through difficult times because you have seen the outcome. Ecclesiastes says, *"Better is the end of a thing than the beginning"* (Eccles. 7:8). Vision works like a prophetic compass to keep us moving toward the picture the Holy Spirit overlaid our hearts with. We are to be transformed by the renewing of our minds that we may prove what the will of God is. The word "prove" in Romans 12:2 means to be able to see what is to come.

When people do not know the will of God, they are disconnected and disoriented. As a result, they only pray the problem without seeing the solution. If the will of God can be seen or proven, then we can pray what we see and not what we feel. When we pray only what we feel, we can only report to God how we feel.

We understand from Matthew 6 that when we pray we are to declare, to see, what is going on in Heaven and look for the same to occur on our turf. Jesus said to let it be on earth as it is in Heaven. When we pray through imagination of the Holy Spirit, we come into agreement with His perspective. A lot of communication fails to qualify as prayer; it is merely venting of frustration. True prayer begins in the heart of God, and He finds people He can plant vision inside who will pray what they envision and not how they feel.

Have you ever been in a prayer meeting where people spent the bulk of the time subverting the vision of the Holy Spirit by painting pictures of gloom and doom? Then in the last ten minutes, they ask God to bless their requests. It seems more like a needs meeting than a prayer meeting. They were not praying from vision; they were explaining away vision.

Jesus asked if He would find faith on the earth when He returns (see Luke 18:8). When Jesus returns, He will be looking for faith, not neediness. He is committed to providing for needs, but needs are not the image we should be carrying.

Use your supernatural vision to connect and stay connected to your heavenly Father, which means living from the inside out.

CHAPTER 6

LIVING FROM
THE INSIDE OUT

*But the Lord said to Samuel, "Do not look at his appearance
or at the height of his stature, because I have rejected him;
for God sees not as man sees, for man looks at the outward
appearance, but the Lord looks at the heart* (1 Samuel 16:7).

First Samuel 16:7 gives us insight into how God sees us and
makes decisions. This is the account of the transition of
Israel's government. Saul was king at this time of change. Saul
had failed to obey God's instructions that came through the
prophet Samuel. Saul was the people's choice, and he governed
by what he saw happening around him. The instructions were
simple; Saul was to wait for Samuel to come and offer sacrifices
unto the Lord before he was to go to war. But Saul became
impatient and observed many people leaving because they were
not willing to wait any longer. Saul, being moved by the sight of

disoriented people and without any regard for the protocol God set for offering sacrifice, offered the sacrifice without a priest or prophet present.

About the time Saul had finished his offering, Samuel showed up very upset at what he saw. It wasn't the people scattering that bothered him; it was Saul doing his own thing. Saul attempted to blame his urgency upon the people; and, when that didn't work, he blamed Samuel for being tardy. Samuel announced to Saul that God was replacing him because of his disobedience. Here is where we get a good look at how God decides matters. Obedience is more than just getting the procedure done; how we do it is the key. Samuel was sent to the house of Jesse to anoint the next king. Jesse lined up his sons and the first one in line was Eliab. Eliab was a big, strapping man, and Samuel thought to himself, "Surely the Lord's anointed is before me because he looks like a guy who everyone would look up to and respect" (see 1 Sam. 16:6). As a matter of fact, he looked rather kingly. Before Samuel could pour the anointing oil on Eliab, God stopped him. The Lord said to Samuel, *"Do not look at his appearance...for God sees not as man sees, for man looks at the outward appearance, but* **the Lord looks at the heart**" (1 Sam. 16:7).

After Samuel concluded the lineup and did not get the release from the Lord to anoint anyone in front of him, he asked Jesse if he had any more sons. Jesse replied that he had one more son who was out tending the sheep, but he was just a boy. At Samuel's insistence, they brought David from the field. David, in contrast to his older brothers, was small and weathered. Yet, Samuel anointed David to replace Saul. David may have not looked the part, but he was God's choice for Israel. God saw something no one else saw—He saw inside David's heart. He saw a willingness to please God, which was a stark contrast to Saul.

The part we should understand from this is that God lives on the inside of all of us. Everything God does starts from the inside. Instead of living from the inside to the outside, most people live from the outside in. Circumstances on the outside can control someone who is not allowing the image of God to break through.

There is a difference between a thermometer and a thermostat. A thermometer registers the temperature of the environment. The thermostat changes the environment to fit the inside of the thermostat. People who live only by what is happening around them, whether on the job or in the home, are reporting only the way things are, not what they could be. If their environment is peaceful and happy, they are happy; if the environment all of a sudden changes, they absorb the environment.

The image God has placed in us is a thermostat and can change the very atmosphere around us. You may have heard the adage that someone is "wearing their feelings on their sleeve." Typically this applies to someone whose mood swings are based on what is happening around them. Happiness is based on happenings, but joy is based on God's image being developed upon the heart.

Truth is what happens on the inside, and fact is what happens on the outside.

Likewise, there is a big difference between truth and fact. Truth is what happens on the inside, and fact is what happens to us on the outside. Numbers 13 tells the story of the twelve spies sent into the Promised Land to see what was there, even though God had told them what it would be like. They all returned to give their objective scouting reports. Ten of them said that there were houses, wells, and vineyards that they did not have to build; but the sons of Anak were so big that the ten spies reported that they felt as small as grasshoppers. They reported the circumstances factually. The last two spies, Joshua and Caleb, said yes to the presentation of the first ten, but then they added that they could easily overtake the giants. Ten of them reported facts; two of them reported the truth.

The truth is what God says. Jesus is the Way, the Truth, and the Life. Facts are merely the circumstances surrounding you, but the truth is what God has declared to be the truth. John 8:32 says that the truth will make you free. Truth is not information, but truth is a person, a person of the Trinity. The Spirit of Truth is called the Holy Spirit.

The only truth that sets you free is the truth you apply.

Learning to live from the inside affects every part of your life. No matter what the circumstance may be around you, you can have peace of heart and mind and a sense that the picture that is inside is not the one you see on the outside. Since they don't match, you have to believe that what is happening around you is not going to define you, nor will it be your destination.

Jesus told the Pharisees in Matthew 23:25 that they were great at cleaning the outside of the cup but left the inside filthy. He was referring to their spiritual lives. They seem to look the part with all their beautiful robes, and yet inside their hearts there was nothing but contempt for the poor and arrogance about their knowledge of the Law of Moses.

God first of all blesses the inside of our being so that it will break through like seed to the outside. Apostle Paul reinforced this thought in Philippians 2:12-13. He says, *"work out your own salvation with fear and trembling; for it is God who is at work in you, both to will and to work for His good pleasure."* Some mistake this passage as some sort of secondary approach to salvation. I believe Paul was teaching that salvation is being worked inside of us until it works out of us. Salvation is a breakthrough truth. Though it begins on the inside as the seed of Christ, it grows until it breaks out so all will see His glory expressed through us.

Made to Express Him

We were not made to just contain Him but to express Him in all that we do. So the salvation that has begun in you will break through the surface, and the outside will be affected by the internal work of grace. The life in you will become the life outside and all around you. What a glorious challenge! And at the same time, it is the work of the Holy Spirit to bring the image on the inside of you to the outside.

The maturity level of believers can be measured by how they live when pressure is applied. They either cave-in when unfavorable news comes, or they consider the opportunities that come from the situation. Mature Christians can change the environment by being thermostats. Mature Christians will change their environment simply by their presence. They can affect their surroundings like a thermostat. Those who are immature will simply do the work of the thermometer, reporting the conditions and attitudes of everyone around them, but unable to change the environment. Be cautious: you can become a sponge and soak up negativity to the point of losing sight of becoming a thermostat.

The Bible says what we see around us is temporary, and the things we don't see with our natural eyes are eternal. The internal can see the eternal, but the external can't see the eternal due to the distractions of the present moment. God has called us to be eternal beings with eternal perceptions. If the only hope that we have is in this life, then we will be very miserable indeed. That sort of happiness is not based on joy. When a person is temporal, their hope is relegated to a temporary moment or a hope in circumstantial issues of time. Therefore, they are happy one minute, and sad the next. Joy is a static place in one's relationship with God. When you spend time with Him and around His people, joy is no longer just an attitude or a feeling. It is God Himself infusing us from the inside out to be able to see what He sees.

For years, I lived my life worrying about what other people thought of me. The worst day of the week was Monday. I despised Monday; Monday was the day when I evaluated everything I had shared in the Sunday message. I was most miserable thinking about the things I should or should not have said, and the things that I did and did not do. Then I had a breakthrough. A seasoned, wise pastor said in passing that he had the same anguish and also beat himself up over each message. He shared the parable about the person who sowed his seed and went to bed not knowing how the seed was growing. Now, instead of digging up the seed, I just go to bed knowing that the seed sown has life of its own and does not need my help to do what it was created to do.

We must not worry about the temporal things; they come and they go. When you set your affection on the things above, it causes something to happen on the inside. It then transforms the outside.

In Matthew 13:18-23, Jesus interpreted the parable He had just taught about sowing seed. Since the culture of that time was primarily agricultural, Jesus used planting seed with an expectation of growing food as a word picture. He described four types of ground to explain the inside condition of hearts. Those listening could plainly see the seed was the same but the soil or heart condition made the difference in productivity. Some seed was randomly scattered on the sides of the road. The birds, being a type of the devil, quickly snatched the seed.

The second type was planted on stony ground that heard the word; but because the heart had no depth, it thrived only for a short time. The thorny heart illustrated those who heard the word, but the cares of life took precedent and it was unfruitful. The fourth heart condition was the good ground. They heard the word, applied it, and produced up to 100 percent.

Living from the inside out is all about the ground you are going to sow into. The external busyness of life can choke out the prophetic picture you carry inside you. Mature Christians will not allow themselves to be pulled into the outside dramas that surround them without changing the spiritual climate. The deeper the maturity levels of the heart, the greater the depth of the Word takes root. If your covenant relationship with Christ is rooted and grounded in love, circumstantial things are less affective in delaying the fulfillment of His promise.

Here is the key to prospering.

Everything God does will begin on the inside of you. True prayer begins inside your heart. Real change in family relationships starts inside the one who has good ground to plant the seed of vision for the new blueprints. If you don't like the fruit you have been harvesting, I suggest changing the seed. Jesus taught that the Word of God is the seed.

There are other types of seed that can be imparted into our ground. The seed of rebellion can take root; and anytime instruction or discipline comes, the heart becomes harder. The harvest is the external result of what has been planted inside. The good news—we can plow up the heart's ground through repentance and plant seed that looks like what you want to harvest.

> *So then, my beloved, just as you have always obeyed, not as in my presence only, but now much more in my absence, work out your salvation with fear and trembling* (Philippians 2:12).

Complaining and cursing is an attraction for every demon from hell. They love it; it is their devil's food cake. Murmuring and complaining works like faith in reverse in the kingdom of darkness.

A great example is in Matthew 8:26. Jesus was asleep in a boat along with some of His pupils. A storm kicked up, and they awoke Jesus in a panic. After rebuking them for their shallow faith, Jesus rebuked the wind, and calm was restored. Jesus had authority over the storm because there was no storm inside Him. The tempests inside will always find a way to the outside at some point. Peace starts on the inside and moves to the outside. We can either attract demonic influence, or we can attract the favor of God. It all depends what is inside the heart.

John captured the heart of Jesus more than anyone else. He was called the beloved in Scripture, and he was also entrusted to write the Book of Revelation. John was seen many times leaning on Jesus' chest engaged with every word Jesus spoke. The other disciples were curious as to their seating arrangements when they entered into the Kingdom of Heaven. They were apprehensive to ask Jesus themselves so they enlisted John to do the asking. John had no selfish ambition working on the inside of his heart, so he could ask Jesus their question without any fear of rebuke.

The condition of the heart either causes us to be apprehensive or to be able to move with confidence. It didn't matter to John where anyone would sit; all he wanted to do was love on Jesus. John had depth, and the seed sown internally was obvious because those around him always knew what was on his heart. When internal peace and contentment are dominant, outward circumstances are less important.

The Good Shepherd

Jesus was stating His purpose for being the Good Shepherd in John 10:10. He said He came so we would have abundant life. Life is not defined as solely breathing in and out. Life describes the full benefit of being a sheep under His guidance and protection, as opposed to being a goat.

There are three elements that the Bible says contain life. Leviticus 17:11 states that *life is in the blood;* Genesis 1 says that there is *life in the seed;* and Proverbs 19:21 says there is *life in the power of our tongue/words.* All three of these elements are choices we have inside of us to make. The blood of Jesus (see Heb. 9:22) brings about salvation. Salvation starts on the inside. The seed is the Word of God, which, when hidden in the heart, keeps us from falling into error. Out of the abundance of the heart the mouth speaks and sets a standard of measurement for reciprocity. The abundant life Jesus was talking about was not about the amount of goods a person could amass in a lifetime. The abundance of life starts with the life that comes from being cleansed by the shed blood of Christ. He removes the internal shame that makes us feel shameful on the outside as well. The abundance of His seed that was placed in our hearts has the potential to come to the full imagination He has for us.

First Peter says that we have not been born again with corruptible seed but from the incorruptible seed of God. The word seed is translated *sperma*, the DNA of God. Just think of it. We come from the best stock in the world. He has given us the choice to have abundance flow through our tongue. The standard of measure we use to bless is the same standard used to bless us. The tongue is the sowing mechanism that takes from the life of His blood and sows His seed so that we reap the benefits. Now can you imagine the capacity you carry inside the storehouse of your heart? Psalm 68:1 says, *"Let God arise, let His enemies be scattered."* Through the power of His blood, and the seed of the spoken Word of God, you have the capacity and capability to be free to imagine the impossible. And finally, Second Peter 1:3 sums up this chapter nicely, *"His divine power has granted to us everything pertaining to life and godliness, through the true knowledge of Him who called us by His own glory and excellence."*

He has placed in the storehouse of your heart everything you need to realize the image He has stamped upon your spirit.

CHAPTER 7

THE POWER OF
THE SECRET PLACE

Barbra was an out-of-state businesswoman who had enjoyed success in the past. When the economy began to weaken, she found herself in a difficult place as she was far removed from the main office. She prayed for the business to grow, but it seemed to be on a downward spiral no matter what she tried. She listed the business with a broker to sell. Time was running out, and the listing had run out as well.

Barbra had recently heard this message of blessing and the power of a godly imagination. She asked the Holy Spirit to give her a vision or a picture of what she should do with her failing business. She took hold of imagining a buyer who would purchase it. She maintained the vision and the testimony that God would supply the buyer. The day before she was going to have to close the doors for the final time, a buyer came forward with a good cash offer—even though it was not listed for sale. In less than a month, the deal was closed, and she came away with a profit from the sale.

There are many, like Barbra, who need to conceive a vision from the Lord that will give them direction and hope to see the fulfillment of their dreams. The key is to put yourself in the best position spiritually to receive what has already been allocated for you.

> *But when you give to the poor, do not let your left hand know what your right hand is doing, so that your giving will be **in secret;** and your Father who sees what is **done in secret** will reward you. "When you pray, you are not to be like the hypocrites; for they love to stand and pray in the synagogues and on the street corners so that they may be seen by men. Truly I say to you, they have their reward in full. But you, when you pray, go into your inner room, close your door and pray to your Father who is **in secret,** and your Father who sees what is **done in secret** will reward you* (Matthew 6:3-6).

Matthew 6:3-6 helps us understand how to receive. These verses describe the secret place. The word secret is translated differently from what we usually think of as secret. It is two words in compound form: *kata* meaning intensity or strength, and *ishkheo* meaning to exercise the strength to prevail. To simplify, secret in this context means the place to prevail. The secret place is an internal place where a picture has been conceived. At the moment you are in the secret place, you are convinced that the image you are seeing in your heart is yours.

The secret place can occur at a time when you are in worship and prayer, those quiet moments when you are not struggling to do anything but be intimate with the Lord. That is when you have dialogue and not just a monologue where you do all the talking and He can't inject into the conversation. The secret place lets you know when you have prevailed, much like Jacob wrestling with the angel. The result of that experience was a name change. The angel asked his name, and when Jacob gave his name, the angel said that he was now to be known as Israel, which means *one who has prevailed with God.* From that moment on, Israel could face anything, including his brother Esau, and clean up his past mistakes.

Prevail, Then Travail

After we have prevailed and have the assurance we have the picture to run with, we are ready at some point to travail. Travail is the process of delivering at the right time what we have been carrying. Some people try to travail and make something happen without first of all having a prevailing experience. It is like a woman trying to birth something she has never yet conceived. We cannot bypass the secret place for the birthplace and expect fruit from the labor.

The psalmist connected this thought when he wrote, *"I would have despaired* [lost heart], *unless I had believed that I would **see the goodness** of the Lord in the land of the living"* (Ps. 27:13). It is important for us to be able to see what we are expecting. I will believe with you as you read this chapter that you will see, from the deepest part of your spirit, the goodness that is ahead of you. Though I am not too keen on steps, here are three practical ways to begin.

Step 1. Define what you are looking for.

Mark 11:24 says that we should believe we have received whatever we desire when we pray. Desire means to crave and have an insatiable hunger for something. Those who pray without any desire or view of what they are asking are only wishful thinkers. Be as descriptive as possible, and use your God-given creativity.

Step 2. Receive the seed for conception.

John 1:1-3 says that in the beginning (conception) was the Word. The Word was God. Without the Word, nothing was created. The process here is to get a promise from the Word of God that will be your seed (sperma) and to meditate on that Word until you can see it. The graphics of the Word of God will give you a view of what you will carry inside you. It is not uncommon in our world of technology for a young couple to send out a picture of the sonogram of their baby to all their friends while the baby is still in the womb. They start decorating the nursery with the colors that fit the baby since they usually know the sex of the child. They are absolutely convinced that a baby is growing inside, and it is just a matter of time until delivery, because they have the picture to prove it.

Step 3. Perceive what you will receive.

First Samuel 1:17-20 is the story of Hannah, a childless woman. It was the Lord who had withheld a child from her. She became so desperate for a child that she prayed and found agreement with Eli the priest even though Eli at first misunderstood her desperation. She left knowing that God had answered her prayer. At that moment, Hannah had a prevailing moment in the secret place. Once faith has entered your heart, start giving thanks that the Lord has heard the cry of your heart. Perceiving the end result is seeing from the point of conceiving into receiving. You have the picture to prove it. First John 5:14-15 encourages us.

*This is the confidence which we have before Him, that, if we ask anything according to His will, He hears us. And if we know that He hears us in whatever we ask, **we know that we have the requests which we have asked from Him.***

Before change can take place in the environment around us, there must be changes in our thinking. Since there must be a seed involved with everything God does, the Word should also be in the forefront of our minds. Acts 3:19 instructs us to repent and be converted so times of refreshing will come from the presence of the Lord. The term repent here is not only about being remorseful over sin, *metanoeo,* but it is to reconsider and change our minds. For some who have never thought well about others or themselves, they will need to repent and change the way they think before they can change the image they have on the inside.

I have counseled people for many years, and some walk away with a piece of advice. But if it does not penetrate their spirits, it will not produce change. If change does not begin inside, it won't bring change to external issues. Sometimes people desire change but are not willing to change how they perceive others. They want their family to change, their work environment to change, and they want everything around them to adapt to them. This perception is wrong and rarely produces the desired results; change begins within first, and perhaps the biggest change is how we see ourselves.

When we perceive through the filter of His image, everything looks differently. Isaiah 10:27 says that it is *the anointing that breaks the yoke* from the neck. The picture is about a slave. He is not free to enjoy a future outside of his bondage. Anointing is translated as fatness. That is not something that sounds too appealing, but in this case it is a must for freedom.

I will draw this picture more clearly for you. The fatness refers to the internal capacity to gain strength so the inside expands to the point where it busts through the external yoke. As I mentioned earlier, I had a fear of failure that made me compare myself to others, which always brought me up short of the bar. My yoke was the fear of people wrongly judging me. In order to break this yoke, the picture of God's love for me had to increase, or become so fat, in my heart and mind so that the yoke exploded into pieces never to be placed on me again. The internal weight of the image God placed in me had to outweigh my perception of how others perceived me. Now I have a picture of myself loving everyone and them loving me in return. That is way better than thinking everyone is against me until they prove otherwise.

> As for you, the anointing which you received from Him abides in you, and you have no need for anyone to teach you; but as His anointing teaches you about all things, and is true and is not a lie, and just as it has taught you, you abide in Him (1 John 2:27).

The internal growth of the true image of God works in cooperation with the Holy Spirit to fulfill the vision. When we become more convinced that what He has placed inside is greater than the yoke, we begin to see the seed breaking through the ground. First John 2:27 reminds us that His anointing abides in us; and this anointing teaches us how to live in the image He has destined for us. Because of His abiding anointing, we know that greater is His image inside us than the image the world tries to put upon us.

Third John 1:2 speaks to the issue of a renewed mind to perceive correctly. It says, *"Beloved, I pray that in all respects you may prosper and be in good health, just as your soul prospers."* John makes the comparison of the soul (we would say the mind) prospering just as other parts of our lives prosper. To the extent that our minds are prospering or growing is to the extent that we will succeed. There must be an agreement that our minds have with our spirits. The image is in our spirits, and the mind should not contradict the vision of the heart. Since faith is the substance of things hoped for and the evidence of things not seen, the mind likes to agree only with things it can see. This is another reason why our anointed imagination must engage to override the natural, visible world.

Sowing and Reaping Abundantly

Second Corinthians 9:6 says those who sow sparingly will find the return sparse. Paul was not addressing the subject of money exclusively; however, money is many times a reflection of our thinking. The command concerning tithe was a type of testing. As a matter of fact, tithe, meaning the tenth part, is the number of testing. How we handle the tenth determines the prosperity of the other 90 percent.

Some may think poverty is only about money, but poverty can include poverty of soul. If there is prosperity of soul, then there is certainly poverty of soul. Poverty is fear of losing something of value. A wealthy person can have an impoverished mind if the person is in constant fear of losing his or her wealth. Because of soul poverty, the person will not risk losing, so the person tends to hoard and withhold from investing. A poverty mindset affects how people invest time and resources into relationships for fear of losing those relationships.

If the potential for life is on the inside of the seed, then we are all living off of the potential of the seeds we have sown. Wherever you are at the present, you are living off of the harvest of your past. If you want something to change, then you must sow something toward that for change to take place. The opposite of fear is love because perfect love casts out fear.

Love trumps fear every time. Sow toward the relationship you want with your spouse. What does it look like? If need be, come with the opposite spirit to see the kind of marriage you want to see. To allow the perfect picture to develop inside, you must not allow a poverty mindset to decide the size of your harvest. Joseph dreamed big; and though his brothers resented him for his boldness to declare it, they eventually benefited from Joseph's dream.

A young woman came for prayer during a time of ministry and asked me to pray that she would find a husband. I noticed she was lacking in grooming and didn't present herself in an appealing manner. I kindly told to her to prepare herself for the kind of husband she was expecting. I asked, "Are you ready for a husband today?" She eagerly replied, "Oh, yes!" My next counsel to her, "Then he will be a lot like you." The realization came over her face, and she said, "Oh, my." She understood that she was looking for someone beyond what she had invested into her own expectation.

Purpose in your heart the harvest you want.

You must purpose in your heart for the harvest that you are looking for. God supplies the seed, but we have to be the ones to apply the seed to the picture we want to manifest. Part of the leadership of the Holy Spirit is imparting the gift of giving. The gift of giving is the recognition of the seed. Recognizing what you need to give in response to what you are envisioning you want to receive is important. The seed may come in the form of blessing others with words of encouragement or giving time to someone who feels lonely.

One apple seed has the potential to produce a whole orchard. The Bible teaches we are not to despise the day of small beginnings, but to just start where you are. Every seed has a picture on the inside of what it can be. Start in the secret place of giving with an expectancy towards receiving.

Supernatural DNA

Remember, you were not given supernatural DNA for diminishing results. He sent His Word and it does not return without accomplishing the purpose for which it was sent (see Isa. 55:11). Remember, you were created in the stamping of the Father, Son, and the Holy Spirit. You carry the resemblance of all three. They agree with the purpose that you would always be increasing in the abundance of God.

That is why it is so important that we see ourselves as God sees us. In Second Corinthians 3:18, the Bible talks about how a man looks into a mirror and sees an image, and he is changed into the very image that he sees. Matthew 6:22-23 really makes this point clear. Jesus says, *"The eye is the lamp of the body; so then if your eye is clear, your whole body will be full of light. But if your eye is bad, your whole body will be full of darkness. If then the light that is in you is darkness, how great is the darkness!"*

Jesus taught that what your eye beholds, the body becomes. When someone holds on to past offenses or beholds them, they will become like the same spirit that holds them. In the same way, someone can hold on to the testimonies of all God has done, and they will become that person.

The beauty of the Lord becomes us. People who behold good things become like what they see. Young boys will watch sports and study the moves on the basketball court and then they imitate what they see. We can decide in some part what we will become simply by deciding what to behold.

Jacob, in Genesis 30:37-39, used the principle of beholding and becoming. He took rods from poplar trees and peeled the bark in such a way that the rods appeared to have stripes. He placed the striped rods in the watering troughs where the flocks came to drink. The flocks stared at the striped rods while they drank; when they mated, the offspring were born striped and speckled. Jacob took the multicolored flock as his profit from Laban.

If you don't like the results your life has produced, then change what you have been looking at. We tend to reproduce what we have been fixed on. Just like the sheep that reproduced the same image that was before them, we too can find similarities in the behaviors of those we allow into our environment on a regular basis. What the eye takes in will eventually reproduce in some form. If pornography is taken in through the eyes, it will manifest in forms of violence and sexual domination and result in perverted images of what God created. Ultimately, it will destroy the family.

Remember the promise God gave to the serpent in the Garden of Eden. He said the Seed of the woman will bruise your head. We know that was to be Jesus. He could bruise the head of the serpent/devil because there was no corruptible intake into His life. Your purity of vision is what the devil is afraid of. When you see what God sees, you will not reap corruption but life, but your life will have abundance. Please don't allow the deception of the enemy to influence you into thinking that it won't happen because "I'm not that bad." First Corinthians 5:6 cautions that a little leaven leavens the whole lump of dough. There is no such thing as moderation when it comes to perverted images that mock the creation of God.

When Jesus spoke to the disciples to feed the crowd of 5,000, they thought that what they saw would be what they got (see Matt. 14:13-21). However, the law of seedtime and harvest applies here, too. What you sow multiplies beyond the original thought or picture. What you take into your spirit doesn't remain the same like the one seed or the one fish or loaf of bread. It moves past the beginning of the little leaven into generational leaven. Faith is a substance, the structure that you stand on for the things that are hoped for. When we allow the image of Christ to be fully formed in us, it grows far beyond the initial encounter.

The mustard seed looks small and insignificant, but when it finds a place to germinate, it doesn't look the same as it did when it was sitting in your hand (see Matt. 17:20). The little boy had only a sack lunch with a few loaves and fish; but in the hands of God, it was more than enough. A widow had only a little oil and meal, but when it was placed in the hands of God, it became more than she thought possible (see 2 Kings 4:1-5).

When corruptible seed is taken in, there is a multiplication that takes place, but it diminishes the potential of the image of God in an individual. It is the diminishing-returns theory. If the devil can get people to accept a diminishing lifestyle, they become slaves to it. Those who have become slaves have little or no expectation from God.

To break through the diminishing mindset and overcome, you have to replace the corruptible with the incorruptible. Replace the destructive with the constructive that builds your spirit and does not defile it. This kind of replacement therapy includes words that agree with God's picture of you. We can replace the bondage with beholding Him, which will cleanse the old images and give a fresh picture of our potential. What you hold, you will behold; and what you behold, you become. The choice is ours.

CHAPTER 8

DISCERNING VAIN IMAGINATION

*For the invisible things of him from the creation of the world are clearly seen, being understood by the things that are made, even his eternal power and Godhead; so that they are without excuse: Because that, when they knew God, they glorified him not as God, neither were thankful; but **became vain in their imaginations**, and their foolish heart was darkened* (Romans 1:20-21 KJV).

I realize that you may have some doubt about the reliability you should place on your imagination. I quite agree with you. Everything that God made that is pure and holy the devil has countered with depravity that confuses what is godly and what is foolish. It would be foolish for us to think our thoughts are directives of the Lord when all the while we are engaged in an alternate lifestyle from what God has ordained for us.

Paul the apostle instructed that we could know a lot about God by looking at His architecture. With creation surrounding us, he said that we still do not worship God as the eternal Creator. Instead, we become vain in our imaginations.

In the beginning of this book, I stated that before Adam gave away his authority to the serpent, his imagination was congruent with his Creator. After his choice was made, Adam and Eve's imaginations were flipped from thinking like God to having vain thoughts. Vain is translated as empty and worthless and sometimes as idolatrous.

The contrast between vain imaginations and godly imaginations must be addressed. We cannot rely on the image placed in our mind if our mind is set upon revenge and destructive thoughts against another or even ourselves. Satan may place so many thoughts of suicide in a person's mind to the point one might think they are doing God's bidding. But the deceitfulness of the heart is not a reason to throw out creative, Godly imagination just because some wackos say that God told them to do such and such when He did not. To say God said something when He did not is to take God's name in vain or to say God's name is worthless or empty.

We can discern a poisonous plant from one that is good for food is by its leaves or fruit. Without our minds being renewed, we are not ready to rely on the images that pass through our minds. The fruit of the Holy Spirit is a good indication of what kind of seed is producing those images.

Calvin came to me wondering why he and his wife were having difficulty. He said he loved his wife, but the intimacy he had anticipated was just not happening. His wife was not comfortable with his sexual appetite. He was fairly versed in Scripture, especially the one about the marriage bed being undefiled. His wife, Sarah, was compliant reluctantly, but had to admit that she did not feel loved. She had noticed a change in his behavior related to their private life. Months later, Calvin suggested other practices that were beginning to make Sarah feel distant from the man she had made covenant with. It was not hard to discern what had changed in Calvin's life. I asked point blank, "How long have you been looking at pornography?" Without any hesitation, he said, "Just recently; maybe a few months ago. I really started when I was younger, but stopped when we first got married."

I explained to him that pornography is an addiction. It takes images of intimacy and turns them into vain, *empty, worthless images* that will never satisfy because they are not from God. I went on to say that Sarah didn't feel loved because to him she was simply an object in a corrupt image that he brought her into. He was able to see that pornography was all about himself and that it became idolatry. This also explained the reason he was having difficulty worshipping the Lord.

Pornography does not stop there; it works like leaven until it is thought about constantly in an obsessive way and vain images replay in the mind. For some, it begins with a curiosity and the thought that one glimpse won't hurt. The same way that God will burn the image of His goodness on your heart is the same way the devil will superimpose his destructive images on your mind.

Then the Lord saw the wickedness of man was great on the earth, and that every imagination of the thoughts of his heart was only on evil continually (Genesis 6:5).

The text goes on to say that God would destroy humankind from the earth. However, Noah found grace in the eyes of God. I find this incredible. The imagination of humankind was at such a fever pitch that all they imagined and thought about was evil. Their thoughts were on everything that God was against; they were all about perverting the creation of God. The devil was having his way with God's creation.

Then, right in the middle of this debauchery is Noah, who found grace in God's eyes. Noah was able to live with an image different from everyone else around him. God gave Noah an architectural miracle. His mind became set upon seeing God's plan of escape. He was ridiculed by those who carried such corrupt images of life that they were too obsessed to even see or hear anything different from the images they embraced as their own.

What a great contrast. One family of eight with a godly imagination was separated from all those who were convinced they were mainstream relevant. All the while, their imaginations were about themselves and not about the God of creation.

God gives us a test for idolatry:

> *It shall be when he hears the words of this curse, that he [an idolator] will boast saying, "I have peace though I walk in the **stubbornness** of my heart in order to destroy the watered land with the dry"* (Deuteronomy 29:19).

Stubbornness is translated here as imagination of my heart. If someone is imagining vain things, they have hardened their hearts against God. When a person who is embracing vain imaginations does not glorify God, they are clearly walking in vain imaginations and stubbornness of heart because they no longer value the things of God.

When discerning vain imaginations, it is important to understand that everything God does *begins on the inside.*

Everything God does from Genesis on starts with a seed. From the origin of one image, things will be multiplied and duplicated. The picture of the resurrection of Christ at the right hand of God can deliver those held in the chains of corruptive images. Just one glimpse of Him in glory causes all other pictures to pale.

When God told us to be fruitful and multiply, He was actually telling us to be full of seed.

While taking an agriculture class in high school, I was given a test at the end of the course. One of the questions: Is a tomato a fruit or a vegetable? My sharp mind of deductive reasoning quickly thought; *everybody knows tomatoes go into salads, so it must be a vegetable.* To my dismay, I discovered that tomatoes were classed as fruit. Fruit is defined as a structure of a plant that contains its seeds. The Bible tells us to go and be fruitful— not go and be vegetables. Godly imaginations will be fruitful when they are full of seed, which is the Word of God.

The test of godly imaginations is simple—the thought always points toward God as the Originator. The thoughts deposited by the Holy Spirit will build up someone and encourage and motivate him or her toward a life that resembles the God of creation. Thoughts that bring people to the knowledge of the will of God will collide with those that are selfish and ambitious and point to the idolater.

Vain or Godly Imaginations

Another way that vain imagination can overtake someone is through unresolved anger toward another person. When a person becomes offended, and they rehearse the offense over and over, it tends to expand and take on a life of its own. The pictures of the offender can become three-dimensional and very graphic. If you begin delighting in the suffering of those who have offended you, then you know you have entered into vain imaginations that are pronouncing curses.

The best test for this kind of imagination is to ask, *Do I want the same thing to happen to me that I have imagined for them?* It is a godly imagination if the thought of blessing them is paramount in your mind. It is an evil or vain imagination if you have only images or thoughts of the person's demise; then you have aligned yourself with the curse and opened the opportunity to receive curses.

It is not good enough just to keep our mouths shut and not say something derogatory. The Holy Spirit also wants to have control over the intents of our hearts. When He is in control of our intents, He is able to be in charge of the images that pass through our minds. There are stories passed down for generations for the purpose of carrying family grudges as part of their legacy—like the Hatfield and McCoy feud. When vain imaginations linger, they block entire families from prospering, because they accepted the grudge as truth and will have difficulty knowing truth when it comes their way.

Maria lived in the Midwest and was ridiculed by family for her business practices. Whatever she did, they let her know it was the wrong decision. Maria took on the offense to the point it brought division in the family, and she went to great lengths to avoid seeing them. She had contempt for them as much as they had for her. She assumed they were jealous of her, and she built a fortress of thoughts around that premise.

When Maria purchased a piece of property, her family made light of it and said she had made a bad decision. After a while, Maria decided to sell the property. Well, five years later, the property was still for sale without any hope of a buyer. Her detractors called her property a jungle and taunted her, "How is the real estate business going?"

Maria said that after she read my book, *The Power of Blessing*, she realized she had been cursing without realizing it. The cursing had given her a picture of disdain for and competition with the other side of the family, and she had clear images of their destruction. She decided to go to the property and speak blessing over it and then she passed by the house of the alienated family she had been cursing. This time she blessed them in the way she wanted to be blessed. She changed the image screen of her mind and tried to consider how God would view them. Before the week was out, she got a call from the former harassing family members and they made her a fair offer on the property they had been cursing. For five years, she saw no results until she saw them through the image of God, not the image that had been created through family offense.

Second Corinthians 10:4-5 teaches us that our warfare is not with flesh and blood but mighty through God to the pulling down of strongholds. We are destroying speculations and every lofty thing that rises up against the knowledge of God, and we are taking captive every thought to the obedience of Christ.

The word for strongholds here is *noema*, which means thoughts. The thought that builds a tower is the one that we build out of vain speculations that trap our minds and keep us from hearing truth. If that speculation does not bring peace or resolution in a family, then a tower remains that the enemy gains an advantage from. We are controlled by what we are imagining the other party is thinking about us. The only action that begets freedom is to stop rehearsing former offenses. The tower comes down when we see what Jesus would do. Get a picture of their success and bless them with the new image, and you will destroy the fortress that keeps sabotaging your breakthrough.

> *For whatever is born of God overcomes the world; and*
> *this is the victory that has overcome the world—our faith*
> (1 John 5:4).

Whatever is *gennao*, born of God, has the potential on the inside of it to reproduce after its own kind. Whoever is born of God will understand that all of this stuff on the outside is a temporary condition. We were born again not with corruptible seed but with incorruptible seed. When we experienced the new birth in Christ, there was an awakening inside us. The word translated as "being born" means to have the ability to reproduce after the seed that birthed us. This gives us all the potential to reproduce the life of Christ, to see life through His eyes, and to expect miracles.

Since Jesus expected to do what He saw the Father do, then we also should train our hearts to look for the opportunities of one born again. The next component of this verse is our faith that leads to the victory circle. To see the picture of someone being healed is only the first step. It takes faith to act upon the image and pray for that person. The Holy Spirit does not show us a picture of a miracle just for information sake—it should prompt us to move in faith. Faith is substance; when a person moves in faith, there is meat on the bone, so to speak, that adds to the vision.

Many visions die on the drawing board because there is a lack of faith to take it to the next level of reality. When a creative imagination is born inside us, it is up to us to give it substance by moving it from an internal thought to sharing it with others who can bring their expertise to the project. The difference between those inventors who are successful and those who have a creative idea is faith in action. Believing is more passive and contemplative, whereas faith moves and makes an idea visible to others.

If we only knew how much the Lord was cheering us on toward completion, it would motivate us to recognize that our good ideas are inspired by God and waiting to be born. Aborted seed is unrealized potential. Someone could not see the benefit due to past failures. Well, this is a new day and old failures have passed away, and you have been born again, and you are now a new species. You are a new model, a species created for winning! Here is how God sees you as Commentator watching over you.

> ***Many,*** *O Lord my God, are the wonders which You have done, and **Your thoughts toward us;** there is none to compare with You. If I would declare and speak of them, they would be too numerous to count* (Psalm 40:5).

> *For I know the **thoughts that I think** toward you, saith the Lord, thoughts of peace and not of evil, to give you an **expected end*** (Jeremiah 29:11 KJV).

We have the mind of Christ when He places His thoughts inside us for the purpose of letting us see the expected end. The end is victory with His image attached.

> *By this we know that we love the children of God, when we love God and observe His commandments. For this is the love of God, that we keep His commandments; and*

His commandments are not burdensome. For whatever is born of God overcomes the world; and this is the victory that has overcome the world—our faith. Who is the one who overcomes the world, but he who believes that Jesus is the Son of God? This is the One who came by water and blood, Jesus Christ; not with the water only, but with the water and with the blood. It is the Spirit who testifies, because the Spirit is the truth. For there are three that testify: the Spirit and the water and the blood; and the three are in agreement. If we receive the testimony of men, the testimony of God is greater; for the testimony of God is this, that He has testified concerning His Son (1 John 5:2-9).

Faith is how we externally respond to our internal response of believing the truth. Anything else short of that is not the pleasure of God nor is it an act of faith. This is the victory that we have in this world, which is to overcome the external stuff. This happens as a result of what happens on the inside of us and results in faith.

What we believe in our hearts determines how we will respond to external circumstances. If we believe Jesus is Lord and have internalized that, then our reaction will be in faith and based upon the truth. What we believe determines how we act.

It is the Spirit that bears witness, and witness means to testify, as seen in 1 John 5:7. It is the Holy Spirit who is verifying, as though you had someone on the witness stand corroborating your story. It is the Holy Spirit corroborating inside you about what Jesus did on the cross.

You know that you have been born again because there is something inside that bears witness that you belong to Him. It is the Spirit who bears witness because the Spirit is truth. The Bible says that God declares that those who do not have the Spirit of Christ within them are not His. It is actually the Spirit of Christ who testifies in our hearts that He has overcome and that we are of the same stock.

The Spirit, the Water, and the Blood

But we must remember there are three that bear witness, the Spirit, the water, and the blood. These three are in agreement. You cannot cause the Spirit to work against the Word. It's not like your mom and dad. Remember asking your Dad for something and he said no; so you went and asked your Mom, and you got your yes? The Spirit and the blood and the Word all work together, and none will contradict the other. So if our feelings are contradictory to the Word, it is not the Spirit of truth. These three always agree.

Sometimes people giving empathy and compassion can draw a person away from the witness of the Spirit. It can make the person miss what God is trying to say in regard to that particular situation. The witness of God is eternal, and it is based on the blood, the water, and the Spirit.

Let's take a look at that for a moment. God is saying that you must be born again. There is a natural birth, a spiritual birth, and a supernatural one. First of all, we have a natural birth. We emerge out of our mother's womb by virtue of the water. Then there is a spiritual birth that takes place because of the blood of Jesus.

In the spiritual birth, the blood of Jesus washes away the sin. The blood does not just cover the sin; it completely washes it away. As a result of this spiritual birth, we are full of the potential for increase, spiritual seed if you will. His seed is from another world. The seed that is now part of our make-up allows us to see from God's perspective, to act upon the nature of God, and to sow from the perspective of God because of vision. It is not only that we can be born by a natural birth, and that we can be born of a spiritual birth by the blood, but we can also be born through a supernatural birth by the Holy Spirit. He wants us to be filled with the Spirit so that the seed that has been planted within us becomes relative to the situation we are facing.

The three that are in agreement in Heaven are the blood, the water, and the Spirit. These three are in sync with one another. They function as one.

- God the Father is the Progenitor, the Creator of the seed.

- God the Son is the Seed of life and the One who sows the seed.

- The Holy Spirit is the administrator of the estate of God. He oversees the seed fulfillment.

God's desire from the very beginning of creation was for us to be extraordinary people. For example, God announced Isaac was going to be the covenant son, not Ishmael. God said He would bless Ishmael because of Abraham, but His covenant was with Isaac.

Covenant is more valued than blessing. Blessing in material things is measured by the temporary value of a carnal mind. Covenant is eternal and is established on the inside of the heart through a strong desire to know God.

Isaac sowed in the year of famine when no one else was planting. Isaac didn't respond to the famine with a normal response, but he responded to the image of harvest God had imposed on his spiritual eyes. The year of the famine, Isaac reaped a hundredfold. It does not matter what the economy does. We can live from the place where God blesses above the natural sequence of events. It is important to note that we must have a different spirit to live in an unseen world called the Kingdom of God.

A great example of this is found in Daniel 6:3. Daniel was taken captive when the Chaldeans captured Jerusalem and took many of the young men for servants. The Bible says that Daniel possessed an extraordinary spirit. He stood out from all the others. He distinguished himself by implementing the gifting God had given him. He was a Jewish young man living in an ungodly culture of idol worship and perversion. But Daniel lived from the inside where God lives. The image he carried was not one of melting into the pagan culture. Instead of the Babylonian culture affecting him, he influenced everything he touched. Daniel 11:32 says, *"the people who know their God...will carry out great exploits"* (NKJV).

When we live according to the influences outside, we tend to absorb the environment around us. When we live from the inside out, we will say and do things from a heavenly perspective. From this heavenly culture we are sowing toward what we believe. Those who have an inside relationship with God will find themselves, at times, moving against the trends of a post-modern culture. But when we do what is on the inside of our hearts, then the circumstances on the outside will change as a result of our obedience.

A few years ago, I prophesied over a young man saying, "You are going to write songs and they are literally going to go around the world. God has seen your heart, and He wants to use you as a worshiper." The kid looked at me and said, "Sir, I don't even play an instrument."

The Holy Spirit said to me, "Did I say it or did I not?"

I replied, "Lord, I believe that You said it, but you heard what the guy said." I left the seed in the ground and hoped the young man would not abort the proceeding word of the Lord.

I was in Houston a couple of years later and a pastor attending the meeting approached me with a music CD. He asked if I recognized the name on the label. I couldn't recall the name at all. To refresh my memory, he relayed the story about the young man who had received the word. The pastor said that the young man wanted to tell me that he is now playing the guitar and had produced a CD, which was doing very well.

The things that are visible are temporary, but the unseen things are from a dimension of the Spirit that is hidden away inside you—just waiting for faith to activate the gift.

CHAPTER 9

THE REAL YOU

The real you is not the person you see in the mirror every morning. The real you is deep inside waiting to emerge into the person you were created to be. Your blueprint has already been designed by the Father, the Son, and the Holy Spirit. They have already imagined you. Now all you need is to allow that design to surface so you can take your place.

For most, at least in the beginning of this metamorphosis, there is a compilation of words that were said to us that framed the image for what we call self. Since words create pictures, and pictures can direct destiny, it is important to differentiate between what the Word of God says about us and what our family said about us. Remember, God's instructions to Samuel were not to judge by the outward appearance, but to look at the heart. Today, we could probably say, "Don't look at a person's clothes or hairstyle." God looks for the real person—the person with whom He can unite His Spirit.

First Corinthians 15:45-49 sheds light into the transformation of the new and improved you. Paul gave us the analogy that

Adam was the prototype of humankind and was the natural or First Adam. Due to sin and disobedience to God, the First Adam lost the place that God had prepared for him. Since God does not give up on what He has imagined, it was necessary to improve the First Adam. God so loved what He had imagined that He sent part of the architect team to be the second Adam. Since there was a part of the second Adam in all of the First Adam's offspring, then it was possible the Second Adam (Christ) could emerge through the First Adam.

What was imagined, that Christ the second Adam would live through the First Adam, fulfilled the original plan of intimate identity. The First Adam was natural, which meant he was created from the earth; but the Second Adam, Christ, was supernatural and came from God's presence. When the supernatural Adam is given complete rule, the real you, as He imagined you, is unveiled.

God only appoints; He does not disappoint.

The author of Hebrews said that Jesus is the express image, the *"radiance of His glory and the exact representation of His nature and upholds all things by the word of His power"* (Heb. 1:3).

The nature that He has imagined for us is exactly like Him. I know that is a stretch for some to fathom. Remember, God does not give up on what He has imagined. He finishes what He begins. We tend not to carry much hope or expectation so as not to get our hopes up and become disappointed. Disappointment is a preconceived idea that it is not God's idea. God only appoints; He does not disappoint. He wants us to live in hope so we will be looking and finding what He brings our way.

God wants to bring out the real you so you can represent Him on earth just as Jesus is representing you through intercession in Heaven.

Clash of the Old Self and the New Self

> *Do not lie to one another, since you laid aside the **old self** with its evil practices, and have **put on the new self** who is being renewed to a true knowledge according to the image of the One who created him* [you] (Colossians 3:9-10).

Paul told us three times in Colossians 3 to put off the old and put on the new. It seems that the only hold up is the conflict for control between the old nature and the new creation or the old Adam and the new Adam. The old nature taught us how to react to negative stimulus instead of acting upon the Word of God. The old self gets offended when feeling slighted and reacts defensively with accusations.

The new self sees things from an eternal perspective so the temporal offense has no power or control. The old nature feels the injustice whereas the new self knows God is just and any injustice here will eventually be justified in the life to come. The new self is created on the inside with the prototype of Jesus. In order for the new and improved version of us to arise, we need to first allow the Second Adam to take precedent and rule over the First Adam.

First John says we have overcome the world because we are from Him (out of Him) and greater is He who is in us than he that is in the world. The old self functions from the surrounding environment; and the new self launches from the eternal peace and security from what is inside. In essence, greater is the new self than the old self. There is an adage that says: whatever you feed the most wins and becomes the strongest or most dominant in your life. If the old self is allowed to go unchecked and is fed a steady diet of agreement, the old self will rule.

For the Word of God is living and active and sharper than any two-edged sword, and piercing as far as the division of soul [old self] and spirit [new self], of both joints and marrow, and able to judge the thoughts and intentions of the heart (Hebrews 4:12).

The old self gets the last word in, but the new self puts in the Word of God by living it out for others to see. Christ is seen as the Word that separates the fallen Adam from the resurrected Adam.

All things came into being through Him [The Word], *and apart from Him* [The Word] *nothing came into being that has come into being* (John 1:3).

Without the Word, there cannot be a new self. The very creation of earth came out of His spoken Word. The new self also needs Him to speak inside us to separate the mindset of this world from the creative Word of God.

The term "old" in connection with the old self is not referring to the age of the person, nor is it gender specific. Old, *polayos* in the Greek text, means it is outdated and not able to expand or grow. New (neos) is the idea of being refreshed and able to regenerate. Something is able extend to the full extent of the boundaries. A good explanation of this is in Luke 5:37-39. Jesus said no one puts new wine into old wineskins, because the new wine will burst the old wineskins, and the wine will be lost. New wine in its fresh state will ferment and expand or stretch the wineskin. Old wine has already reached its peak of fermentation and expansion and no longer presses the wineskin to expand.

The reason Paul exhorted that we should put off the old nature is because it cannot grow into anything more—it has reached its potential and can't extend beyond its own will. The old self sets its will against growing in the Spirit. The old nature rebels against any suggestion of submitting to God's purposes.

For instance, we are encouraged to put on the garment of praise. Could there be the opposite effect of a garment of cursing? This tells me that we have to take off one garment in order to wear another one. We cannot wear the garment of praise (see Isa. 61:3) if we choose to wear the garment of cursing.

The real you, that Christ sees, wears His identity and emits praise for the greater One who lives in you. Paul said that the hidden mystery is Christ in you, the hope of Glory (see Col. 1:27). Hidden away inside you is the greatest adventure of your life and also the greatest potential realized. When the new self is no longer hidden but emerges, it will be a game changer. The new self carries hope because Christ is in you. The old self has no hope and is not expecting anything but failure and cynicism because the old self wants to be in charge and will use only carnal thinking to make decisions.

Called, But Your Choice

In Matthew 22:1-14, Jesus taught using a parable about a wedding feast that was prepared by a king in honor of his son who was to be married. The guests were those who had relationship by ancestry with the king; in this case, Jesus was referring to the Jews or the covenant people. Those invited in the first round of invitations made excuses of one sort or another and claimed to be too busy.

This is a great picture of what the old nature does when there is an invitation to encounter more of the Lord. After declining the invitation, the king sent out a second invitation to anyone who would come, no matter their background. The wedding room was filling up when the king saw a man who was not wearing wedding clothes. It seems a little confusing that the King kicked out a guy who was not dressed up when he invited anyone who would come.

Those hearing the parable understood it, because it was a Jewish custom that everyone was given a wedding garment when they entered the banquet hall; it was to be worn over the clothes they came in with. The garment usually had the king's crest woven into the garment. Everyone who came in would wear the identity or insignia of the king. The crest on the garment would speak of the conquests of the king and all of his dominion. The man was not thrown out for what he wore to the event, but because he refused to be covered with the new identity of the king's son. He wanted all the benefits of the king's feast while maintaining his own independence from the king. Likewise, there are a lot of people who want to marry Jesus for His money, yet want to keep their own identity, their old nature. This man wanted to eat free food, but not wear the garment that praised the king and his son.

The real you must take on a new identity—that of King Jesus, the Son of God. He has wonderful benefits to share with those who are covered by His blood, which gives us true identity for eternity. The saying, "the clothes make the person" comes to mind relative to the real you. What we are clothed with determines what kind of person will emerge. The parable also reveals that the man who was exiled from the wedding celebration was sent out into darkness; when someone rejects Christ, he or she is sent into darkness, eternity in Hell, and is separated from God. It is not enough to be invited to join Him in an eternal Heaven but one must also enter into the celebration covered with the garment of forgiveness that only His Son can provide.

Jesus finished the parable with a final comment that many are called and few are chosen. We could also interpret this that few will choose. The calling is an RSVP in response to the King. The potential of being in the presence of the King was not realized by those who received an invitation. Then there are those who might respond, but when they come to the point of entering and realize there is a requirement of laying aside their identity to take on the representation of the King of Glory, it goes against their old nature. The will of the old self has to surrender to the will of the King to enter into the benefits of His marriage.

The Bride Has Made Herself Ready

Let us rejoice and be glad and give the glory to Him, for the marriage of the Lamb has come and His bride has made herself ready. It was given to her to clothe herself in fine linen, bright and clean; for the fine linen is the righteous acts of the saints (Revelation 19:7-8).

This bride was responsible to make herself ready for marriage. She had to choose to wear the linen. Linen represents purity, but also the acts or choices she makes. One way we put on the new self is by choosing to do the right thing even when it is not the easiest choice. The more the real you walks out the righteous acts of a bride who has made the choice to please the one she adores, the more the old self will disappear. Paul said, if we walk in the Spirit, we will not fulfill the works of the flesh. Since the old self is the flesh, we can conclude that the Spirit helps the bride focus on her betrothal so the old nature cannot insert its ugly input.

The Real You Wins!

> *For by these He has granted to us His precious and magnificent promises, so that by them you may become partakers of the divine nature, having escaped the corruption that is in the world by lust* (2 Peter 1:4).

The promises that are made to us by the Word of God are extraordinary. The promises are only made to the one who has become a participant in the divine nature of Christ. Those who have chosen to keep their old identity are not eligible for the benefits of the King's Son. Notice the change in natures. The old nature is not aligned with His divinity and becomes a partaker of lustful, worldly corruption. The *real you* receives the new nature and it is a divine one—the nature of a new creation engaged to the Son, the Last Adam, and we will reign with him forever.

One reason some are frustrated by not seeing answers to prayer is because they want to keep their old identity while asking for the promises of God. Answers to prayers are reserved for those who have put on the wedding garment and entered the divine nature, those with the DNA of a life filled with great joy and provision.

The Key to Becoming the Real You

Beloved, now we are the children of God, and it has not appeared as yet what we shall be. We know that when He appears, we will be like Him, because we will see Him just as He is (1 John 3:2).

The word appear was used three times in this chapter of First John. It was used in two different ways. Two Greek words were used: *phanero* and *epiphanero. Phanero* means to shine brightly with the idea of revealing. The second word, *epiphanero,* changes the tense to present. We know that one day, when Jesus returns for His Bride, we will be caught up with Him and changed in a twinkling of an eye. However, in the present tense it means to be changed right now. This excites me greatly, because the verse says that as He appears to me right now (present tense), I will be changed into the revelation I am beholding.

For instance, when someone gets revelation that God is the Healer, then that appearance or revelation brings about healing. As He appears to us, we are changed into His image from glory to glory. Beholding His goodness causes us to become better at living life here, while we wait for the change that will occur at the end of the age when our bodies will be changed. Right now our hearts are being changed to fit His image. The more we see Him through Scripture and testimonies, the more we become like Him.

First John 4:17 says *"...as He is [right now], so also are we in this world."* No more procrastination for me; I don't have to wait to find real change. I can have it now in this present world. All I need is to have an encounter with Him through the ministry of the Holy Spirit. The Holy Spirit is the Spirit of Truth, so His job description is to unveil what has been hidden in this present time, which is Christ.

Right now, allow the Holy Spirit to flood your mind with His love and goodness. Ask Him to fill you with the hope of His appearing. You can be filled with the Holy Spirit as you are reading these pages. Don't let the old self talk you out of receiving your promise from the Father.

CHAPTER 10

SEEING THE UNSEEN

I was in fifth grade, in Mrs. Caldwell's art class. Art did not come to me naturally. I would much rather have been outside playing football, which was more of a natural instinct. I asked my teacher why I had to learn art, since it had nothing to do with the four Rs. Besides, I was embarrassed about my lack of ability, so I just figured art class was for sissies. The only redeeming fact was that everybody, including the jocks, had to take the class. She replied in a way that made no sense to me at that time. She told me that art helps you get in touch with what you can't see. My comeback was, "Well, if I can't see it, maybe I'm not supposed to see it. And if I can't see it, then I can't draw it." I couldn't draw a straight line with a ruler.

Mrs. Caldwell passed out some drawings and asked, "What do you see in this picture?" All I could make of it was that a 2-year-old must have spilled paint on the paper. All the brainiest classmates saw trees and buildings, which told some story. Boy was I ever lost. I felt I was among aliens and the teacher was the droid that directed them. Obviously, I had no appreciation for art, because I did not have an eye for it. It took awhile, but years later I started seeing differently. Up to this point, I paid no attention to the world around me in any kind of detail or descriptive way. Now when Diane asks me if I like what she is wearing, I can honestly have an opinion. It is possible to develop sensitivity to what the Holy Spirit wants to show us. At first, it may look very abstract and confusing, but keep asking Him for truth in what you are looking at. There are many things that escape us daily because we are focused on the external and not trained to see through the eyes of the Spirit.

> *Do not lose heart, but though our outer man is decaying, yet our inner man is being renewed day by day. ...while we look not at the things which are seen, but at the things that are not seen; **for the things which are seen are temporal, but the things which are not seen are eternal*** (2 Corinthians 4:16-17).

This Scripture passage may smack of science fiction a bit, but it really is not. It is only that we have not really thought about it in this context of spiritual reality. Apostle Paul contrasted what we are so accustom to seeing all the time to what is eternal and unseen, and yet the eternal or unseen things are very real. I know there are whacky folks who try to make something spooky out of this passage. The reality is that physically we are diminishing daily. As we age, there is less of a lot of things and more of the stuff we don't want. Paul wants us to see that we are moving *toward* the eternal value that is not always easy to see.

> *Where there is no vision* [ability to see], *the people are unrestrained* (Proverbs 29:18).

When people are not able to see any direction beyond the confines of their routines, they are unrestrained. Unrestrained in this context means they are not attached to anything that is going forward. When there is no ability to see the unseen potential in a spouse, a marriage can falter. When we see the eternal things that are not seen at the moment, we can go through difficult times of confusion. The picture that the Holy Spirit has developed and glued to your heart allows you to see the end result.

Leah is a very talented and gifted musician and worship leader. I have known her since she was 18 years of age. She carried the desire in her heart to release the songs the Lord had given her into a recording. Though she had plenty of encouragement from friends and even me, it didn't seem to be enough. After hearing this message on the Power of Imagination, one evening while getting ready for bed, she had a flash of what the CD cover would look like. That picture, or image, moved her to take steps to gather the other musicians and start the process of recording her desire.

Just One Picture Away

Many people are just one picture away from fulfilling a long-time-in-coming dream. If a picture is worth a thousand words, then we should stop talking about it and start looking to see what it will look like and move toward the blueprint. Start with what you know, and the details will follow.

Most parents display their children's artwork on the refrigerator and make a big deal over the Crayola smudges drawn to express their love. That same childlike faith still exists inside you, and when you choose to express those images on the inside, you are expressing your love for God, who designed you with that creativity.

Some things are difficult to see because of their magnitude and the distractions that tell us it is impossible. When we see from the inside out, and don't measure the probability from the circumstances screaming at us from the outside, we are better able to succeed.

Jesus found it necessary to retreat from the crowds to get alone and pray. I suspect the dialogue He had with His Father in Heaven brought a view of things to come and set a course that would not be aborted. When Peter strongly disagreed with Jesus about going back into Jerusalem, Jesus had already seen the path He was to take. He turned to Peter and strongly rebuked to the spirit motivating Peter to dissuade Him: *"Get behind Me, Satan...you are not setting your mind on God's interests, but man's"* (Matt. 16:23). The Bible says that Jesus' face was set toward Jerusalem. He had the image of God's plan, and nothing was going to distract Him from His destiny.

Jesus answered a question from his disciples about a parable he had taught:

> *To you it has been granted to know the mysteries of the kingdom of God, but to the rest it is in parables, in order that seeing they may not see and hearing they may not understand* (Luke 8:10).

Jesus was referring to the "religious people" who were unable to see. Parables are stories that parallel reality. A story is used to give a graphic illustration of a truth. Jesus used stories and examples that related to farming, land, and nature, as Jewish people commonly understood these things. Their imaginations allowed them to see at the level of their faith. Due to their religiosity, some were blind to the reality of the parable.

The Holy Spirit will also give you thoughts that paint a familiar picture, which allow you to connect with the bigger reality of what He wants you to see. Religiosity interferes with being able to see plainly. The Pharisees were spoken to in parables, but Jesus told His disciples they were granted the privilege to hear plainly the mysteries of the Kingdom of God. The Kingdom is all around us; and in fact, Jesus talked about the Kingdom of God being at hand. Jesus was the expressed image of God and His Kingdom; yet the proud, arrogant, and religious people of the day could not see the Kingdom at hand. Their backgrounds and traditions would not permit them into the place of seeing beyond their boundaries.

My definition of vain traditions is truth-addition. People tend to take elements of truth and add their own flavor and perspective so that they control the image to which they are conformed. There are those who create a Jesus who is made into their image. They add what fits their lifestyles and superimpose Jesus (truth) over that image; and voila, they have created another god without power and authority to deliver them in times of trouble.

The Kingdom of God is not just something we believe is out there in space; the Kingdom of God daily demonstrates the attributes of our King. We carry His image on the inside, so we can see those hurting and know He is present to heal. The religious people talk about the Kingdom, but those who do not need parables to have their eyes opened are living in the reality of His Kingdom here on earth.

In Matthew 16:18, Jesus announced to Peter that He would build His church and the gates of Hades would not overpower it. Notice the word He used for hell was not Sheol but Hades. There is a difference. He said *gates* of Hades, meaning more than one gate. Sheol is actually the place of one gate. There is one gate in and one gate out of Sheol. Sheol is the place for the devil and his dark angels and for those who reject the Son of the King who rules and reigns through His Son.

Hades means that which blocks the light. We could say anything that blocks out the revelation of Jesus could be a gate of Hades. A good friend who keeps you from attending a time of worship could be a gate of Hades. A sporting event that comes before honoring and worshiping God could be a gate of Hades. A gate that causes the image of Christ to be changed into a pseudo facsimile of the real Jesus is a gate of Hades.

One of the reasons some have trouble seeing the Kingdom of God is because they have lost the divine picture in their hearts of the King of this Kingdom. It takes the component of light to be able to see anything natural or spiritual. Jesus is called the Light of the world; and then in Matthew 5, He tells us we are the light of the world. He expects us to see what is happening in the unseen world of His Kingdom because we have light. When a gate of Hades has blocked the light, we lose sight. After a while, being blind to His Kingdom, His will being done on earth just as it is in Heaven, we become more sensitive to the kingdom we are building, which without Jesus, the gates will overpower.

The unseen world we call the Kingdom of Heaven moves at the speed of light. Humankind measures the speed of light as 186,000 miles per second. The angels are angels of light, so they move at this speed or faster, beyond what natural eyes can see. Movies move at about 24 frames per second; x-ray machines operate at about 30 frames per second. This speed is beyond the ability of the eye to see. In order for an angel to enter the earthly domain, I would suspect they would have to slow down considerably before anyone could see them. Just because I can't see them moving is not evidence they don't exist. We may be able to discern their presence, but the natural eye cannot see them. My point is simple. It takes spiritual eyes to see the Kingdom of God, which is very real but is not a natural kingdom. To see natural things, I can use my natural eyes; but to see the invisible Kingdom of God, I need spiritual senses to cooperate and synchronize with His domain.

It is the glory of God to conceal a matter, but the glory of kings is to search out a matter (Proverbs 25:2).

The Lord really wants us to be able to see what He is doing. Something that is concealed is only hidden from those who don't want to use the energy to search it out. We are to be hungry kings and queens, who will not stop until we see what we are searching for. There are times God will hide something from us to start a pursuit. The pursuit unveils many other aspects about Him that He wanted us to see, which would not have been discovered if we had not been searching.

God Speaks

In 2009, God told Wendy she was going to have a baby girl. Wendy began the usual steps of preparing for the arrival. It had to be steps of faith because Wendy was having difficulty conceiving. The Holy Spirit told her to do the things she needed to do if she knew she was pregnant with a girl. She thought, *Well I would be buying lots of pink, frilly things.* Wendy saw signs on the back windows of cars stating Girl Onboard. Every sign pointed her to see a baby. She said, "I knew I was to speak things that appeared not, as though they were to be." Her journey began by telling the first person, her husband, Jim. After some interesting conversation with Jim, he was onboard.

Other friends were informed as time went by. Wendy recounted how close she felt to God during these steps of faith. She knew her biological clock was counting down; she was already 39 years of age. On Mother's Day, she found out she was pregnant. Wow, was she elated; she told all her friends. Her dream was on its way. But three weeks later, she had a miscarriage. Though she was very sad over the loss of the baby, she did not feel a loss of the promise that God gave her. After some recovery time, she discovered she was pregnant again, only to have a second miscarriage three weeks later. This time the pain was more than she thought she could stand. The year 2009 went by and there was no baby.

After a trip to Africa, the Lord opened her eyes to the insurmountable number of abandoned children. She knew the promise, and all the signs she had been standing on about a baby girl, but now she was open to adoption. Three months later, a couple living ten minutes from her home became pregnant. They knew they could not financially support another child in their already expanding family, so they wanted to put the baby up for adoption. Though Wendy did not know if the baby was a boy or girl, she knew this was her promise. Wendy and Jim's great joy was realized when the birth parents announced the baby was a girl. Though the final piece to Wendy's picture was concealed, she understood more about God's ways by searching for the fulfillment of God's promise to her. She perhaps would have not had the revelation of God in that way without the journey of pursuit.

The writer of Hebrews encouraged us to fix our eyes upon Jesus who is the Author and Finisher of our faith (see Heb. 12:2 NKJV).

When challenged by circumstances that seem to contradict what you have been envisioning, fix your gaze upon on the One who authored your faith to believe the vision. While standing in faith for the fulfillment of your expectation, it is crucial to keep your eyes upon Jesus who was also tested but was faithful to the heavenly vision.

CHAPTER 11

DEEP CALLS TO DEEP

Deep calls to deep at the sound of Your waterfalls; all Your breakers and Your waves have rolled over me (Psalm 42:7).

We know that God created us from His imagination or determination, and He determined we would not be a shallow people. In Psalm 42:7, the psalmist was expressing his thirst for God in the middle of adversity; to deal with the opposition, he needed to draw from the depths of God.

The deep the psalmist wrote about is his spirit encountering God in the way that Adam did in the Garden of Eden when God's Spirit would move through the Garden and Adam would know what He was saying without any struggle to communicate. Our spirit does not have trouble recognizing God's voice and direction when we allow the deep to commune. Our minds are made to store history and information to function in the seen world; but without renewed minds, our rational thought process blocks the deep things of God from entering our gates.

Worshiping in the Spirit opens the gates and starts a dialogue with the depths of God. Paul says that the natural mind is carnal and is at enmity with God. When the mind is trained to submit and come under the truth of the Word of God, then the mind will be a servant and not the master. The mind will always be in conflict with the deep things of God. Though it is normal for our spirits to crave the presence and the depth of God, it seems foreign and strange to an un-renewed mind.

Before the fall of mankind, Adam was directed and instructed by his depth or spirit. After the disobedience and the removal from Paradise, everything was reversed. Instead of being dominated by his spirit, now Adam's mind was in charge of processing God's will. Unlike the spirit, the mind takes in all the surrounding circumstances and uses the natural senses to draw conclusions as to what it will believe and allow into our lives. This makes it difficult to release the imagination God intended for us to have so we can see things from His perspective.

Adam was to oversee and take dominion in the Garden, but when he gave up his ability to have Godlike imaginations, he lost the strength to take dominion. Now, much of dominion is done out of carnal minds without the resource of God's image being in our forethoughts. The good news is that our minds can be renewed to come under the leadership of the Holy Spirit through recognizing His place in the formation of our lives.

Jesus said that when the Holy Spirit came, after He ascended to the Father, the Holy Spirit would guide us into truth. Truth is not information; truth is what Jesus is saying. Jesus is still speaking to us today through the depths of the Holy Spirit to our spirits.

When He had finished speaking, He said to Simon, "Put out into the deep water and let down your nets for a catch" (Luke 5:4).

Jesus was beginning to choose His disciples, those who would turn the world upside down. He came to some fishermen, primarily Peter, and began to talk to him about a subject with which Peter was familiar, fishing. Jesus did not begin by expounding the principles of Kingdom living or any other theological treatise. Inside the discussion there was the message of the unseen.

Jesus began with a command to see if they would respond. He told them to move the boat out farther into deeper waters. Peter's first response was to give a rational explanation about what they had already done in the past 24 hours without any results. Peter started his journey as a follower by expressing his mind, with all of its data-gathering capability, by saying, in essence, "We have fished all night and have caught zip." I am sure in Peter's experienced fisherman's mind was the thought that now was not the right time to fish. His experience told him the natural conditions were not favorable for catching fish and, they should put it off for another day. Our minds are notorious for procrastinating, eager to push things into the future without any urgency for the moment.

To his credit, Peter recognized Jesus was not just another Rabbi after he had listened to his teaching. Peter responded, *"I will do as you say and let down the nets"* (Luke 5:5). Peter was on his way to training his mind to submit to higher authority, even if it went against natural reasoning. It is worth noting that Peter said, "I will" let down the nets. You can make a case that the nets represented what he was in control of—his mind and will. Once he submitted his nets, or will, to the command of Jesus, everything changed from that moment on. When they moved from the shallow water to where Jesus had challenged them to go, a miracle took place. The nets were so full of fish they began to break. The abundance led them to bring in their partners; so now their obedience not only prospered them, but it brought others into the encounter as well.

> *He said to Simon, "Launch out into the deep and let down your nets for a catch"* (Luke 5:4 NKJV).

The word deep in the Greek is *bathos*. Bathos means that which can't be seen with the natural eye. It is not visible with a casual glance. Jesus' message was beyond just fishing. It was about following Him into a life that would not be visible at first. It is a life that you will only be able to see through your spirit and at times will be in conflict with your mind.

The psalmist cried out for his depth to communicate with God's depth; this is a normal desire of your spirit and for someone who has learned how to submit his or her mind to a higher authority. Peter became one of the greatest apostles who followed Jesus. Though at times Peter seemed to let his mouth and mind dominate his person, eventually he learned that it was not his will but only God's will that should be done.

> *Others* [seed] *fell on the rocky places, where they did not have much soil; and immediately they sprang up, because they had no depth of soil. But when the sun had risen, they were scorched; and because they had no root, they withered away* (Matthew 13:5-6).

In the parable of the sower and the seed, Jesus showed the concept of longevity when there is no depth of good ground for the seed to germinate. Though the seed and sower were good, it is obvious the problem was with the shallowness of the soil. When testing came, as seen with the sun, the seed quickly died. The Word of God is good seed and is only effective to the depth it is sown. When you witness someone who begins serving God with great zeal and then shortly burns out, it is an indication of a shallow heart; the seed was not sown deep enough to develop roots.

> *...that He would grant you, according to the riches of His glory, to be strengthened with power through His Spirit in the inner man, so that Christ may dwell in your hearts through faith; and that you,* **being rooted and grounded** *in love, may be able to comprehend with all the saints what is the breadth and length and height and depth...* (Ephesians 3:16-18).

The ability to imagine all God has for us takes us to search the depth of His Word so we don't walk in a vain imagination. Depth keeps us from confusing natural vision with supernatural vision. Where there is not much depth, the lines become blurred because we still want the security of the shallow end of the pool yet desire the adventure of the deep. The next verse ties this thought together. Ephesians 3:18 shows that the reason for the strength of the inner self is so we may comprehend the breadth and length and height and depth. These four dimensions are beyond the natural eye's ability to accurately perceive; but when we see things as a visionary, these dimensions start to fill in the blanks—and the vision of God's blueprints take on a structure of faith.

When you imagine something that is abstract, it may not be enough to launch on. Keeping this in mind allows the other added dimensions to give it shape. Eventually depth overtakes shallowness, and the picture is sure and steadfast and will pass the sun test and not wither.

We Serve a Prophetic God

God is prophetic. That means He wants to speak to you about your future. The devil, on the other hand, wants to remind you of your past. God says He has given you a hope and a future, not a hope and a past (see Jer. 29:11). When you hear a voice telling you of the marvelous future He has planned for you, you can know it is not the devil trying to discourage you by reminding you of past attempts and failures.

The future is dependent on us being able to see, hear, and know the Lord's intentions; and the more we allow the Holy Spirit to add depth to us, the likelihood we will fail or quickly rise decreases. You may have come from an environment where you were (or currently are) constantly told that the best that you can ever do is where you are. You may have developed the mindset, or the mind picture if you will, that nothing good will ever happen to you beyond where you are at the moment.

God says that *"eye has not seen and ear has not heard, and which have not entered the heart of man, all that God has prepared for those who love Him"* (1 Cor. 2:9). The strength of the vision is tied to the depth of the love of God. We should not, however, put the love of a vision above the love for the One who gives vision. Abraham had to pass the love test to receive the promise that his generations would inherit the Promised Land. After Abraham took Isaac, the promise of God, to the mountain to offer his son as an offering, then God said, *"Now I know that you…have not withheld your son, your only son, from Me"* (Gen. 22:12). God wanted to test Abraham to see if the gift of Isaac was more valuable than the Giver of the gift.

The vision we carry will be tested to ensure we are not substituting the gift over the Giver. Vision is delayed when we stop worshiping God. When the baby (vision) is loved more than the father of the baby, idolatry can be developed in the absence of God being worshiped.

> *Jesus answered, "My kingdom is not of this world. If My kingdom were of this world, then My servants would be fighting so that I would not be handed over to the Jews; but as it is, My kingdom is not of this realm"* (John 18:36).

Jesus was living more in the reality of His kingdom than the reality of this world. If we could understand as He did, that our kingdom is not the temporal one that surrounds us, we would not be disappointed in this earthly realm. Jesus was speaking of a Kingdom that was beyond the natural eyes but is very clear to those who see with their spirits.

Pilate questioned Jesus as to the proof of His Kingdom. Pilate was thinking in terms of an army and a castle, things all earthly kings identify with kingdoms. Jesus told Pilate that His kingdom, His dominion that the Father had given Him, is not of this world. He said if His Kingdom were of this world, then His servants would be fighting. In the natural kingdom, a king must have an army, and that army must be at war to keep the kingdom. The reason Jesus announced that his servants were not fighting is because the war is not of flesh and blood but of spiritual principalities that influence the natural kingdom against the spiritual kingdom (see Eph. 6:12).

154 THE POWER OF IMAGINATION

Where your kingdom is, there will be your place of warfare.

People war where their kingdom is. There are wars and rumors of wars because people are trying to establish kingdoms here upon the earth. Where your kingdom is, there will be your place of warfare. In order to operate in the Kingdom of God where the King of peace, the King of glory, and the King of all authority resides, we must operate in the realm of His Kingdom. The Kingdom of God is not set up in the same manner as ones upon earth.

Some people are naturally empowered because their personality is so strong and dominating. They won't take no for an answer. The power that they operate in is of a natural variety and not the supernatural. They can get things done simply by pushing and pressing to make them happen.

Jesus was standing in a supernatural capacity and the realm everyone else lived in was one of unbelief and selfishness. We are, however, in this physical realm that is so slow that everyone can see it. We consider it to be real, and it is real to the natural senses, yet the reality of His Kingdom is real to those with faith to see it.

*Therefore Jesus answered and was saying to them, "Truly, truly, I say to you, the Son can do nothing of Himself, unless it is something **He sees** the Father doing; for whatever the Father does, these things the Son also does in like manner"* (John 5:19).

Jesus told them that He could do nothing unless it was something that He could *see* the Father doing. Some have always thought that Jesus was referring to an impression. He was not talking about His physical eyesight, but rather what He saw in His Spirit.

The word image does not mean we look like God. It is the same word used in the Scripture from Genesis that describes how man was created in the image and likeness of God. The concept is that one can literally see the glory of God by looking at the creation of God. It is an image or facsimile of God. When someone looks at you, they are seeing the image, the facsimile, of the glory of God. So Jesus said He could do nothing on the earth unless the likeness of the Father was showing through. Jesus laid His deity aside when He came to earth to take upon Himself the likeness of man so the likeness of God could break through into this world.

God's Likeness

I was on a plane flying somewhere to speak when I felt the Lord prompting me with a quick glimpse of a woman in my mind, and somehow I knew the woman had stomach cancer. When I arrived at my destination and got up to speak, I took a quick survey of the audience to see if I could pick out the woman. I didn't see anyone who even remotely looked like what I had envisioned. I thought I must have misunderstood, even though I saw her clearly! I knew precisely what she looked like, but I simply did not see her.

Then on Sunday evening, the woman came up to me during the service. I had prophesied to her husband earlier in the morning, but I had not seen her. She said that she had not been in the earlier meetings due to stomach problems. She had been to the doctor, but no one knew what was wrong. She said, "I am losing weight and I am sick all the time." Then the Lord said to me, "There she is." I did not tell her that it was cancer. I simply prayed for her. I was able to feel the virtue that flowed into that woman. Because I had already seen the healing, it was already done. It was already completed and now was in the process of manifesting in the realm we live in.

Once we are able to see it, then we are also released to walk it out just as we saw it. If we see it, then we are responsible to be obedient to do what we see. So Jesus was saying that He was not operating from this earthly realm but from another Kingdom. He was operating in a manner just as He saw it. The Father loves His Son, so He showed Him all the things that He was doing.

Remember the prophet who was so prophetically correct that he was telling the secrets of the Syrians and they wanted to kill him? The host of the Syrian army was on every side of him posed to overtake him. The prophet wasn't bothered about it at all, but his servant certainly was. Two men looked at the same thing, yet they saw something totally different. When the prophet's servant started to panic, *the prophet asked the Lord to open his eyes, so he could see the invisible kingdom.* When the servant's panic in this realm gave way to the reality of the Kingdom of Heaven, he was strengthened. He saw the whole hillside filled with the host of Heaven, with the angels ready to defend them against the Syrians.

Fear is like having a dirty window; it obstructs your vision when you are trying hard to see beyond the physical realm into the window of Heaven. When the servant saw the host of Heaven, and that it had been there all the time, his reality changed from being fearful to knowing that greater is the kingdom not seen than the kingdom we live in. The situation did not change in light of that insight, but the response of the servant changed once the truth was revealed to him.

If you do not react to your situation out of fear, then the devil has no way to attack you. Fear is a sign to your enemy that you are falling back.

Call deep unto God and He will be with you through every situation.

CHAPTER 12

HEALING THE ORPHAN SPIRIT

I will ask the Father and He will give you another Helper,
that He may be with you forever; that is the Spirit of truth whom
the world cannot receive, because it does not see [behold]
Him or know Him, but you know Him because He abides with
you and will be in you. I will not leave you as orphans;
I will come to you (John 14:16-18).

In John 14, Jesus gave us the promise of the Holy Spirit; we won't be abandoned. The sense of being an orphan is a feeling of no hope, and survival is the single issue of every day. An orphan has no sense of future, much less any inheritance. The feeling of loneliness can grip someone while in a crowd and even among people with whom they are acquainted. Carrying an orphan spirit causes people to see things through the filter of abandonment.

In some very impoverished countries, the orphans are many times the ones in the streets without supervision and scantily clothed. Some of them do not even know their legal names because they have no record or recollection of their parents. The legal definition of an orphan is one who has no parents or family. Jesus promised to replace the feeling of being an orphan with the presence of the Holy Spirit. The Holy Spirit would not only be with us but would live inside us. It is the Holy Spirit who helps us see what our hope and future looks like. Without the Spirit opening our imaginations to see what we can become, we will take on the orphan spirit and feel blocked from any potential that is ours.

The replacement for Jesus was not a different Spirit than what He displayed while among them. Jesus was physically with them, and it was not difficult for them to follow Him. They could follow Him using their natural abilities. They could follow Him while thinking about something else. When Jesus ascended to Heaven, they felt somewhat abandoned. They no longer could use the eyes in their heads to see Him. It would take a whole new type of vision—but just as real—only in another dimension. It was no longer the eyes in their heads; now it was the eyes of their hearts that would be exercised.

The disciples had relied so much on Jesus to hear God for them, and to pray for their provision, that they felt all alone when He ascended. What potential they thought they had was gone because Jesus was gone. They felt like orphans because they didn't recognize that the Gift did not leave them, but would actually become closer than before. In fact, the Holy Spirit would become so close that they could not see Him but could sense Him from an internal perspective.

I know the feeling of seeing where I need to go but not knowing how to get there. While driving to a hotel in a rental car in Los Angeles, I could see the high-rise hotel in the distance. I was feeling confident that I could see my destination. Right before I could see the sign showing me the exit number, a truck pulled alongside and blocked my view of the sign. The blind spot caused me to miss the exit. I drove a few more miles, exited, and circled back to look for the sign. I saw it this time, and it read two miles ahead. Now I felt safe again, knowing I would be in the right place in just a few minutes. About the time I was close to the exit, I received a cell phone call, got distracted, and passed the exit again. Though I had the hotel in sight, I could not get there. The third time was a bust as well. I thought it lunacy to be so close yet realistically so far away. A ten-minute drive turned into a half hour of frustration. I felt lost driving in circles, while I watched my destination come and go repeatedly.

Adults with orphan mentalities lose sight of long-range plans and settle for getting their needs met in that the present moment. Another mindset that spiritual orphans have is being accustomed to someone giving to them. They are fixed on what someone else can do for them. They get comfortable with their conditions and settle into accepting life as is. Though you may not have the outward signs of an orphan, you may notice the signs in thought. But consider this:

> *For all who are being led by the Spirit of God, these are sons of God. For you have not received a spirit of slavery leading to fear again, but you have received a **spirit of adoption** as sons by which we cry out, "Abba! Father!"*
> (Romans 8:14-15)

If you are having trouble living from the inside and trusting what the Holy Spirit wants to show you, then you can get healed right now as you read these verses from Romans 8. Your adoption is the adoption of your spirit. The part of you that is eternal. Though the external circumstance doesn't appear to be any different, your spirit is not an orphan and there is no need to feel abandoned. You are set to see with a new lens.

Proverbs says that we become what we think. If we think like an orphan, we will be treated like an orphan. Some who carry rejection will soon find out the issue was due to an orphan mindset, and orphans don't trust people. They are accustomed to living in a protected cocoon.

In order for the power of imagination to be effective, you must recognize the indwelling of God to release the envisioning of God. You are not abandoned; you are in partnership with the Holy Spirit. The Holy Spirit moves in an environment of truth. Abandonment is not truth. It is a lie the devil plants in the thoughts so you won't trust the insight of the Spirit.

> *Now we have received, not the spirit of the world, but the Spirit who is from God, so that we may know the things freely given to us by God, which things we also speak, not in words taught by human wisdom, but in those taught by the Spirit,* **combining spiritual thoughts with spiritual words** (1 Corinthians 2:12-13).

The Holy Spirit in you confirms you have rights as a true son or daughter to know what is freely given to you, not as an orphan or beggar, but as a child of God. An orphan spirit blinds us to the truth of all that God has for us who have eyes to see it. The power to imagine the Father comes from being a child who trusts his or her father.

Fig Leaves

Then the eyes of both of them were opened, and they knew they were naked; and they sewed fig leaves together and made themselves loin coverings (Genesis 3:7).

Adam and Eve became self-made orphans. They chose to disobey God and to thus break ties with Him and His name. They went from eating the tree of life to eating from the tree of the knowledge of good and evil. They became orphans by knowing more about evil than enjoying the trust and peace of God. In the Garden, the only covering they had was the glory of God. Their bodies were covered by the glow of His glory. They saw each other through the lens of glory. They were not aware of their nakedness or any lack.

When the glory left Adam and Eve because they abandoned God, not because God abandoned them, they became aware of their new status as orphans. They had no Father covering them. By their own need, they took leaves and provided their own covering for their nakedness. Orphans feel vulnerable that someone will see their nakedness and take advantage of their weakness. Those who carry an orphan spirit tend to cover themselves with extra work or other substitutes. When we provide our own covering, it is difficult to see our destiny because we have cast off our heritage of a child dependent upon the Holy Spirit for guidance.

After Adam and Eve rejected God's covering, they heard the sound of God walking in the Garden, something they had experienced many times before. However, this time the sound did not draw them close; the sound of God moving among His creation caused them to hide. If you ever feel like running in the opposite direction when faced with opportunities to encounter God's presence, you might be living with an orphan spirit. It is amazing how in a moment's time Adam and Eve went from enjoying God's presence to feeling unworthy to be seen by God.

I can relate to some degree of shame. When I was a teenager, I was spending the night with a friend who lived across the street. I thought I had taken care of the requests for the sleepover. I had done this many times before over the years, so it wasn't any big deal to me. Late into the evening, my dad, whom I loved dearly, called the neighbor to say I did not have permission to be there. I argued my thirty-second mantra that Mom knew I was there, but I headed home. As I stepped into the house, Dad was standing behind the door waiting for me with his favorite belt.

As he attempted to swat me for arguing with him, I grabbed the belt out of sheer reaction and said, "I'm too old for this anymore." I thought to myself, *I'm dead meat now,* and I couldn't even look up at him. There was a moment of silence, and I chanced one eye and looked up at my dad. I saw a hurt, teary-eyed father. He quietly said, "Go to your room." All night I saw the hurt on Dad's face. I had never seen him break like that. I realized that I had rejected his covering as a father. I felt so low and ashamed. I felt like I did not even belong to the family in which I was born. I could not wait until the next day when I heard his truck pull into the driveway. I had to tell him I was sorry and I would not reject his discipline again. He graciously accepted, and I felt the weight of the world leave me and a sense of belonging covered me again.

Orphans want the covering but will reject the discipline. At times, orphans roam from one covering to another, dodging any sense of belonging and avoiding discipline. Hebrews 12:6 tells us that God disciplines those He loves. This teaches me that if I reject the discipline of the Lord, it isn't discipline I am rejecting but the Lord of the discipline. When orphans cast off the moorings of the Father, they lose the inheritance that was ordained for them.

Self-made Orphans

Many examples have been drawn from the parable about a son who took the inheritance of his father and squandered it on riotous living (see Luke 15). The son came to the end of his irrational behavior and realized he had nothing and was living in a pigpen. Though he still carried the name of his father, his circumstances placed him in the category of living like an orphan. His father was wealthy and longed for him to return; the prodigal was not enjoying the benefits of his heritage. Finally, the son came to the end of his shame and decided to return to his father's house even if it meant being a slave.

Many can identify with this young man's condition. We know that God, our heavenly Father, can do anything, and He has an infinite supply of what we need. But when we can't see ourselves being any more than living at the mercy of what others will do for us, we continue to carry an orphan spirit. Like Adam and Eve and the prodigal son, we too can become self-made orphans by not realizing what we have been given.

> *...that there be no immoral or godless person like Esau, who sold his own birthright for a single meal* (Hebrews 12:16).

The Bible describes Esau as godless because he despised his position as firstborn son. He could have had the double portion of his father, but at a moment of desperation, he sold it for a bowl of porridge. The Bible says that God hated Esau mainly because he devalued what he had. A spiritual orphan won't realize the benefits of what they have been given. Their self-assessment always makes them feel needier than they really are. Orphans get so focused on their lack that they rarely volunteer to help others. They usually think about how they can benefit by the situation they see around them. Esau's lack of understanding of who he really was caused him to think only about satisfying his own hunger and immediate need.

The entrance of the wounding can be the entrance of the healing.

The healing of the orphan spirit is often related to being wounded by someone in a place of authority. Spiritual orphans often feel exposed when a person of influence should have been covering them. Trusting some leaders may be difficult, but that is where the healing can begin. The entrance of the wounding can be the entrance of the healing. An orphan heart will be reticent to trust again. If they are not able to trust those in authority, then they will be hindered from entering into a desired vision. Orphans who will not allow healing to come will find it difficult to imagine anything but rejection, so rejection really becomes the expected norm for them.

Orphans often oblige the situation by rejecting leaders before anything good or bad occurs. The cycle continues until the orphan, like the prodigal, comes to the point of recognizing their true identity as a child of God and not a wounded outcast. The vocabulary of an orphan usually includes, "I don't know where I fit" or "I feel like the square peg trying to fit into the round hole." It becomes natural for orphans to find reasons not to fit in. Healing from a wounded soul allows spiritual orphans to see the good and not just pick out all the bad.

When Jesus came into the place called Solomon's porch, He saw a paralytic waiting for someone to place him into the pool when the angel came down and stirred the water for a miracle. Jesus asked the man, "Do you want to be made whole?" The man avoided the question by reciting his usual practiced response. He said that he didn't have anyone to help him into the water at the precise time. He further explained that many times someone else would get in before him and cut him off from his miracle. The sad picture here is the man did not hear Jesus' question; he heard out of his orphan heart of positional rejection. Jesus asked about healing, not for an analysis of the conditions surrounding his life. Orphans tend to miss miracles because they are used to making excuses for their rejection. Instead of saying, "Yes, I am ready to be healed," they make excuses.

Perhaps the United States is on the verge of entering into an orphan spirit. When we cast off the moorings of our Founders, we orphaned ourselves from what they had imagined this nation would be; which is one nation under God, indivisible, with liberty and justice for all.

Lord, I ask You to reveal Yourself as the Father to every person who identifies with an orphan heart whether a natural orphan or a spiritual orphan. Open their eyes so they can see the heritage You have imagined them to have. I pray that none will come short of Your glory. I stand and proclaim healing to any who have felt wounded by a person of authority in their life. Let forgiveness be given toward those who have been the offenders. I ask this in Jesus' name. Amen.

CHAPTER 13

WHAT DO YOU HAVE IN YOUR HOUSE?

..."What do you have in the house?" And she said, "Your maidservant has nothing in the house except a jar of oil"
(2 Kings 4:2).

The story in Second Kings is a remarkable testimony of a woman who was the wife of a prophet. Her husband had died, and there was such debt that she was on the verge of the creditor selling her two sons as slaves to pay what was owed. Elisha, a prophet, did not take time to ask why this happened or to offer sympathy. He asked her one question, as if to ask her to give him something to work with: "What do you have in the house." What *do* you have—not what do you *not* have.

Many only have inventory of what is lacking in their lives and do not take the time to see all that they do have. The widow said she had nothing but oil. In her mind, there was nothing in her home that would solve her problem. An orphan spirit is looking for a hand out, while God is looking for faith.

Without the gift of imagination, we overlook the substance God would use to change conditions and to open windows in Heaven. Imagination is creative. The creativity that God designed in us is part of our DNA. Due to living in a fallen world, most people lean toward the panic side of life instead of leaning toward the miraculous side of imagination. Elisha was looking for something that he could be creative with, while the widow was looking for a little relief to pay the bills. Even God used dirt to form man. Faith is the substance of things hoped for. Elisha saw the oil as substance; she saw the oil as the end of her family. The end of something could be the beginning of something when we see it through our God-given imagination.

The end of something could be the beginning of something when we see it through our God-given imagination.

Elisha instructed her to act upon his word by going and borrowing other containers that would hold the oil. The extent of her capacity to make room for more oil would be the extent she had for prosperity to come. After she borrowed all the vessels she could find, she began to pour what she had into other vessels and the oil continued to flow until all the vessels she had borrowed were full. She paid off her debt and lived on the rest. As long as there was room to pour, there was a flow of oil. It is very easy to become so familiar with our lives and routines that we don't see the substance that God has put into our lives for multiplication.

In the late 1990s, I was asked to go to Cuba with some Costa Rican friends to minister the refreshing of the Holy Spirit which was being poured out in my church at that time. In Cuba, we were taken to the far end of the island to teach a group of pastors very discretely. It was dangerous to have open meetings unless the Cuban government had recognized them. We were told that we had to bring food for the small group we would be ministering to. We were told to expect about ten people plus ourselves, which totaled four. We bought a live chicken and few pounds of rice and beans. It was enough for about 15 people.

By the time we reached our destination, it was close to midday. The hosts for the gathering lived in a small house that consisted of two rooms. They started lunch for the guests. Everyone was very hospitable and excited to see what the Lord would do. I noticed people started gathering outside. They came out of the jungle and everyone seemed to know each other and was welcomed. After being introduced, we soon realized these were pastors of house churches that were secretly meeting in various places. The crowd began to grow until we had doubled the original expected number.

During the time when people were arriving, I heard various stories about how different ones got in trouble with the government for killing their own cow or goat for food. Under communism, the government owns everything, so if you kill your goat, they consider it stealing from the government. Because we had bought the chicken from a government-sanctioned store, we were OK.

The crowd had grown to 40 people, and I am not sure how many children were there. Most of them were used to eating one meal per day. I told our hosts to go ahead and feed everyone else; our group could wait until we returned to our hotel. They seemed to be somewhat offended. The interpreter quickly said that the hosts insisted that we be served first. The small house could only seat four people at a time. After we had a portion of chicken with rice and beans, we moved out so others could come in. I stayed near the little burner used to cook the meal. I don't know how it happened, but they kept dipping into the pots of food and the same amount of food remained in the pots. This process continued until the last person was fed. Only then could I hear the spoon scraping the bottom of the pot. I was amazed and obviously excited. They saw my amazement and said, "This happens all the time. We have to believe God to supply or we don't survive."

I realized the Cuban Christians didn't inventory the supply; they simply offered to God what they had as an offering and He multiplied to fit the need.

Is there something in your house that you have become so familiar with that it has lost its value? There are inventions and creative ideas locked up inside all of God's children. There may be a millionaire inside you. Don't compare yourself to someone else who has an easier time of living and conclude they are blessed and you are not. See yourself with the same substance that God gave you when He breathed into you and said it was good. There is life in every seed on the inside that is waiting to be planted. Complaining blocks your ability to see your potential. Complaining is like faith toward the devil; praising God is faith that leads toward a change of mindset so you can see that what you have in your house is there for a purpose.

Hebrews 3:6 says we are the house of God if we belong to Christ. The miracle may not be in the house you live in—it may be in your spiritual house. Inside your spirit is the ability to see and imagine what you are looking for. Once you see the picture, then you know what you are to be looking for. If you don't know what you were created for, you will not give yourself to that which is creative. Many times families have nothing to look forward to because they are not looking forward. They are either looking down or looking backward.

As mentioned previously, God is very prophetic. He is always talking to us about our future—and the enemy is always reminding us of our past. Ultimately, it is the one that you listen to that determines the direction you will go. In Revelation it says that John turned to see the voice. How do you see a voice? When God speaks, it is not intangible; it is tangible and causes us to turn to see what is happening. So when we hear His voice, we turn in His direction. Whatever gets our attention usually turns our head in that direction.

When we have nothing to look forward to, we find ourselves reflecting back upon the past. Whatever you give your attention to will take energy and focus from you. Whatever report you believe, you will find yourself following after that report. So much of Scripture is about whom you believe in and whom you follow after. You can move through difficulties, and you can move through problems, but your heart must be set upon the Lord. God wants us to develop our spiritual senses so that we can know His presence and download His thoughts.

> *...seeing that His divine power has **granted to us everything** pertaining to life and godliness, through the true knowledge of Him who called us by His own glory and excellence* (2 Peter 1:3).

Peter gave a complete statement that everything has already been granted (not given) to us—everything that is relevant to life and being godly. There is a difference between something given and something granted. Granted implies that something is made available to us in a general way. Imagination is built into us so we may see the things granted (though not realized) in the natural realm. There are two biblical terms that apply here: imputed and imparted. It was *imputed* to Abraham for righteousness. It was *imparted* when Abraham acted in faith and proceeded to offer his son as an offering. Imputed means it is available but not received as yet. Imparted means you have taken your part into your being.

There are many who read about the promises being imputed to us and never take the next step of moving in faith toward the promises. God is looking for faith on the earth, not sin. Faith is the response we have toward what has been granted. For instance, someone could call me and say, "Kerry, I have placed ten thousand dollars in your account at the bank." If I go to the bank and request to see the money and withdraw it, they would ask to see some identification. I would tell them, "I am the guy who has ten thousand dollars in your bank." Though I am near the money, I have to have the right identity to receive it. To receive the blessings of the Lord, my identity is through Jesus the Son, and I must confess and show through my life that He is Lord. It is granted to all of us to have everything necessary to prosper and be in health, but we have to be identified as one of His.

My next question: if He has given us everything that we need, where is it or where do we go to receive it? The answer: it is in our house. We are the temples of God. Every promise we are looking for is locked up inside us, waiting to be recognized as the seed of God. When Jesus was speaking to the woman at the well in John 4, He told her that she would ask him for a drink if she knew who He was. The gift could be right in front of us and we misinterpret what is happening. At first, all the Samaritan woman was thinking about was based on her tradition and culture. She was wondering why a Jewish man would be there in the first place because the Jews had nothing to do with the Samaritans. I wonder how many times we missed God's gift because it was wrapped in an unfamiliar package. Perhaps we have dismissed the package because it was not the way we would expect it to be delivered.

Jesus was not received by the religious of His day because they were looking for the Messiah to come through a different tribe, preferably the tribe of Levi. Levi was the tribe where all Old Testament priests came from. Since Jesus came from the tribe of Judah, He was not viewed as one who could possibly be the Messiah that the prophets spoke of. God brought a gift wrapped in Judah, and they were too blind to see their gift. One day, the whole nation of Israel will recognize this gift and turn to Christ, their Messiah.

Deuteronomy 8:18 says it is God who is *"giving you power to make wealth, that He may confirm His covenant which He swore to your fathers, as it is this day."* Notice He did not say I give you power to *get* wealth but to *make* wealth. Some who carry an orphan spirit are looking for someone to give it to them when God gives *us* the creative imaginations that can make wealth. The making of wealth takes acts of faith and an imagination that can see the end from the beginning; whereas waiting to get wealth requires no faith and no imagination and the end results are based on wishful thinking.

As mentioned previously, Matthew 14:16-17 is the account of Jesus feeding the five thousand. The disciples wanted Jesus to send the people away because it was time to eat and there was no provision for them in the place where they had gathered. They told Jesus that there were only five loaves of bread and two fish among them. They had taken inventory of their assets and concluded that they didn't have what they needed to feed that many people. It seemed like a no-brainer to everybody except Jesus. Jesus knew that the amount of food was not nearly as important as the recognition of what God wanted to do. The small little lunch was a substance to multiply. When Jesus blessed the food, He was not telling His Father how small the offering was, but thanking Him for the results that He saw.

Imagination is not denying the present but seeing the blessing.

Imagination is not about denying the present situation but seeing the product of blessing. Jesus saw the end result. He was not just hoping for a few to get fed; He saw the multitude completely fed. The disciples looked at the multitude and saw only the size of the crowd in comparison to the size of the five loaves and two fish. Imagination does not use math to decide whether to believe God or not.

Imagination sees and the spirit confirms the joy that is going to follow your faith. The question we should answer for ourselves is what have we to offer as substance, what are we speaking blessing over? The ability to recognize the potential that may be in our hands right now is important. It is the key that will unlock the destiny that is waiting for your impartation.

Does No Really Mean No?

In John 2, the first miracle of Jesus is recorded. The setting is a wedding in Cana. When the wedding celebration ran out of wine, Jesus' mother requested her Son's help with the problem. Jesus responded that His time had not yet come, meaning that the time for Him to display His glory had not come. His mother didn't take that response as a no, because she told the servants to do whatever He told them to do. It is amazing to me that Jesus said he was not released to do anything; however, when His mother instructed the servants to follow His lead, things changed. Jesus instructed them to fill the six water pots that held thirty gallons each. When the "water" was poured out, the headwaiter was surprised at the quality of wine. The shift from "My time is not yet" to "Fill the pots with water" was one of faith, Mary's faith in Jesus. Jesus needed faith to act on. The water simply was the substance that He used to change natural to supernatural.

Your Answer Is the Game Changer

In Mark 7, a Syrophoenician woman came to Jesus asking Him to cast the demon out of her daughter. Jesus, referring to the traditions of the Jews regarding Gentiles, said it was not good to give the bread belonging to the children (Jews) to the dogs (Gentiles). What she said next was the game changer. She could have gotten offended or returned with some insult, but instead she said, *"Yes Lord, but even the dogs under the table feed from the children's crumbs"* (Mark 7:28). Did Jesus change His mind, or was He looking for something He could work with? Jesus said, *"Because of this answer, go; the demon has gone out of your daughter"* (Mark 7:29). Her answer was the substance Jesus used to move upon to bring freedom to her daughter.

Faith is substance, and it is even in our mouths. When our mouths are filled with doubt and complaining, it becomes substance abuse. It takes the gift and turns it against what we are looking for.

When Jesus is at the door of our hearts knocking, He is waiting for an invitation to perform His will. We can see in the transition from the Old to the New Covenant that the tradition in the Old Testament often caused people to only see the outward through their religious duties, whereas Jesus saw their hearts. At times He jumped over religious traditions into the moment when they gave Him faith to work with, or the miracle would wait for another day.

Imagination helps us look past the veil of religion and see what the Holy Spirit really wants to do; He is waiting for us to give some substance. I remember hearing a testimony about the ministry of James Hudson Taylor. He was an English missionary to China in the late 1800s until the end of his life in 1905. Taylor said, "China is not to be won for Christ by quiet, ease-loving men and women...The stamp of men and women we need is such as will put Jesus, China, [and] souls first and foremost in everything and at every time—even life itself must be secondary."[1]

During one of the missionary trips among the islands, Taylor was resting aboard a sailing ship when the wind stopped and there was a dead calm on the sea. The ship started drifting toward an unfriendly island with probable cannibals hoping for dinner. The captain alerted Hudson to pray. Hudson replied that he should raise the sails. The captain quickly gave the reasons why one does not raise the sails when there is no wind. As I remember the story, Hudson said if there were no sails there would be no prayer. With time running out and the welcoming committee on the beach, Hudson began to pray and wind began coming in great force and pushed the ship back out to sea. Though they had sails on the ship, they were not in use. If the Lord had brought the wind while the sail was down, there would be nothing for the wind to blow upon.[2]

This a great example of those of us who pray for the wind of the Holy Spirit to blow, and yet we have our sail furled up waiting on God to do something miraculous. What will we offer as substance so the Holy Spirit can identify it as faith and blow upon it and change the circumstances from perilous to miraculous?

About ten years ago, I was feeling a need to prepare for the future of my family in a more substantial way. I had been told as a young preacher that God would provide, so I didn't need to think about retirement—and that it was better to burn out than rust out. Years later, some of those with cute clichés were barely making it living on Social Security. I started studying stewardship and realized it was about being entrusted with the wealth of another. The wealth belongs to God because none of us can take it with us when we leave this world, but we sure can pay it forward as a faithful servant when we get to Heaven.

Remember

As I was praying about this, I had prophetic pictures of land and houses. In the Bible, I would read about people who would fight to keep the land and fight to hold a hill of lentils. The Bible talked about the field where the great pearl was hidden. I thought, *OK, I get the picture, Lord. Now, what am I to do with what I am seeing?* I felt that the Lord asked me a question, "What do you have that is your greatest asset?" The verse in Proverbs came to mind about how valuable a good name is. I had always paid my bills and had a high credit rating. I saw that I could purchase property during a time when it was easier to invest in property. The property has become lucrative for a future time. If we take the veil off our eyes as to how we have always approached opportunities, we will not be left out in the season of leanness. Learn to plant in season so you will have abundance in times of leanness.

> ...*having eyes do you not see? And having ears you do not hear? And do you not remember when I broke the five loaves for the five thousand...?* (Mark 8:18)

Jesus asked three questions of His disciples: did you not see; did you not hear; and, did you not remember? This was to say, *I have been doing all these miracles for you to note so you can do these same things.* He told them that He saw what the Father was doing, and that the time would come when they would do even more because He was going to return to His Father.

Wow does that ever hit home! The miracles were not just about meeting the needs at the time, but they had a far greater reach. The disciples were to learn by hearing and seeing and remembering all that He had done. We are to do the same. The old adage that it is better to teach someone to fish than give them a fish is true. Giving someone a fish will only last till he is hungry again. Teach him to fish and he will never be hungry again. I think the message here is to keep alert and give attention to what is happening, because there is a lesson coming out of the need that is greater than just getting the need met and moving on.

Ten lepers were healed, but only one returned to give praise and glorify God for the healing. Jesus told the one healed, "...your faith has made you whole" (see Luke 17:19). This makes me wonder, did the other nine keep their healing since He told the one who returned that his faith made him whole or complete? Perhaps the other nine settled for just getting their immediate problem fixed but did not get the complete or whole package Jesus wanted to give.

The neediness of soul can settle for less than the imagination of the spirit can see. An unthankful heart won't see, it won't hear, and it won't remember. When the next opportunity comes, they won't know how to approach the Lord for their miracle. Imagination is not given to us just as a source to feed from; it's more than that. He gives us eyes to see where we can advocate for someone else who needs wholeness spoken over his or her life.

Ask the Holy Spirit to help you see what you perhaps have overlooked and to bring back to your memory what you need to remember. What you need may have already been spoken, and what you need you may have already been seen, and you need only to recognize it.

But we have this treasure in earthen vessels, so that the surpassing greatness of the power will be of God and not from ourselves (2 Corinthians 4:7).

We are encouraged to recognize that we are not just survivors in this sea of humanity, but we are vessels with a treasure. If the treasure is unrecognized, then the potential that we have been entrusted with has been lost. Though you may have been born into a family with hard ground and little natural resources, you can still rise to the image that has been photographed on the inside of you.

...the god of this world has blinded the minds of the unbelieving so that they might not see the light of the gospel of the glory of Christ, who is the image of God (2 Corinthians 4:4).

There is a god of this world known as the devil that is all about blindness. He attempts to block the light of who you really are. It is the unbelievers who accept the dark ideas and the dark thoughts they carry about themselves and others. When the light of the real image of God through Jesus Christ breaks through the darkness, we can see the picture clearly and resolutely.

God's Light and Glory

I was told the testimony of a woman who had stage four cancer in her abdomen. She was taken to an art gallery to see a local artist who was prophetic in his art. He portrayed the glory of the Lord in abstract ways that only those who had an eye for glory would understand. The afflicted woman was looking at the painting and seemed fixed upon the piece of art. The more she looked, the more she wanted to look. She was drawn by the depiction of God's light and glory. She realized days later that she was completely healed and set free from cancer. She saw something that caused her image of Christ the Healer to be magnified over the cancer. She was caught up in the beauty of the Lord. The Healer inside her was always there. She carried the treasure of His glory. When she caught sight of the true image of His goodness, everything paled in comparison.

Jesus, the image of God, is superimposed upon your heart. That picture alone causes your soul to be awakened to a world you did not realize existed. You have been transformed into this image from glory to glory, from one unveiling of Himself to the next unveiling. In Romans 3:23, Paul says that many have sinned and come short of the glory of God. He did not say that they sinned and missed Heaven; he said they came short of the glory. Glory is the only way you can describe the life that you see through darkness and recognize that Jesus is the only Way—not only to Heaven but the only way to glory in this world.

The very first thing God confronted when creating the earth was darkness. The darkness was the absence of God or glory. He said, "Let there be light." I find it very interesting that God said let there be light and there was light that separated the darkness in Genesis 3:1. Then in verses 14 and 16, the sun, moon, and stars were created. So what was happening in verse 3 that brought light? I tell you it was God Himself who released His glory, and the darkness was pushed back. The natural lights were put in place after that.

The same Light that confronts has also placed light in those who are carriers of His glory. Glory was present at creation when God created man. Adam and Eve carried glory inside and out while in the Garden of Eden. Their bodies did not need clothes because the glory was their covering. Jesus came to restore us to a glorious place where the glory is not just on the inside, but we also wear His glory every time we exhibit His image in faith and kindness.

In Him was life and the life was the Light of men. The Light shines in the darkness and the darkness did not comprehend it (John 1:4).

The light on the inside of us shining out is not a myth. When someone dies, the light leaves their body. Matthew 5:16 says, *"Let your light shine before men in such a way that they may see your good works, and glorify your Father who is in heaven."* Light represents the life of the body. So we could say, let your *life* be so expressed that others would take notice of the light of your Father in Heaven. When we act in love toward someone who is not returning our love, we are exhibiting light and repelling darkness.

Every time you choose to bless and not curse, you are letting the glory light leak out and something happens to your sensitivity level of the Holy Spirit—it increases. Paul told his young trainee that his senses would be more skillful through use. Like any muscle that is used builds strength, to build strength in hearing the Holy Spirit there must be attention given to how to live His image on a daily basis.

Though evil is always present, we can train our minds to always choose light. The Bible says whatever is not of faith is sin. Sin comes short of glory. If it is something that the Holy Spirit cannot use as a substance of faith, then it falls short of glory. Glory is always present when faith is released; and darkness is present when the choice is made without the advancement of light. Light always proceeds ahead of us or else we would be lost and stumble. Glory is always ahead of us showing the potential for the miraculous.

Jesus said in Matthew 6:3 that when you give alms to the poor, don't let your left hand know what your right hand is doing. We sometimes hear this verse being used during an offering at church. The word hand was not used in the original translation from the Greek. It says don't let the left interrupt the right.

It is worth noting that science is clear about how the brain works. It is divided into two hemispheres the right and the left. The left side is for calculations and math. It is where we weigh evidence before making a decision. It is the rational part of our thinking. It also is the part where skepticism comes from and doubt originates. From the right side of our brain, comes the emotional part that is romantic; and we are more likely to use the right side for faith thoughts as that is our more intimate side. I suggest to you that Jesus was not referring only to hands but to our thinking as well. We could perhaps say that we are not to let doubt and unbelief control us, but let faith take us into the place of generosity.

Let's be generous with the poor, generous with thanksgiving to the Lord. Jesus sits on the right side of God—the side of authority and power. In Matthew 25:33 Jesus says at the end of the age when the nations are going to be judged that He will send the goats to the left and the sheep to the right. Goat thinking goes to the left and sheep thinking goes to the right. The mind of Christ is the mind that will stay on the right side of His throne.

According to Romans 12:2, I pray that you will be transformed by the renewing of your mind; and that you may prove what the will of God is, that which is good and acceptable and perfect.

Amen.

Endnotes

1. Christian History Website, "Hudson Taylor: Christian History," http://www.christianitytoday.com/ch/131christians/missionaries/htaylor.html, (accessed November 10, 2011).

2. Eugene Myers Harrison, "Missionary Biographies: J. Hudson Taylor: God's Mighty Man of Prayer," http://www.wholesomewords.org/missions/biotaylor3.html, (accessed November 10, 2011).

You may contact Pastor Kerry Kirkwood by:

Email: kerry@trinityfellowship.com

Website: www.trinityfellowship.com